alec

the King Canute Crowd

eddie campbell

eddie campbell comics

2000

ALEC: THE KING CANUTE CROWD
First printing February 2000.
Published by Eddie Campbell Comics,
PO Box 230, Paddington Q 4064, Australia.
email: camp@gil.com.au
Book designed by Michael Evans.
PRINTED IN CANADA.
Available in the US from: Chris Staros,
Top Shelf Productions, PO Box 1282, Marietta GA 30061-1282.
Internet: www.topshelfcomix.com
ISBN 0 9577896 0 2

PUBLISHING HISTORY

About half of the total material here appeared masquerading as short stories in a number of British small press comics such as **Flick**, **Fast Fiction** and **Escape** between 1981 and 1986.

It was collected in 30 page volumes nearly equivalent to the "books" in the current edition, by Escape Publications, these three were published in 1984, 1985 and 1986. The proposed fourth failed to appear.

Everything was collected in one volume by ACME/Eclipse in 1990 with Book 2 expanded to 39 pages and Book 3 to its current 32. For this reason it was titled **The Complete Alec**, even though my own title had always been **The King Canute Crowd**, a fact which I announced in print as early as 1983. The material was again printed in parts within my monthly **Bacchus** comic between July 1996 and January 1998 where Book 2 was re-edited with a much lost material reinstated and presented in its current size of 48 pages.

Author's preface...

...in which he perhaps has a last chance to prove himself superior to the naive young fool who started the book twenty years ago. Intent upon capturing all the nuances of tone in the emotional life he found around him, he aimed to get it all down, no matter how odd or silly it seemed. It is autobiographical, of course, and was envisioned at the onset as a *novel*, though we weren't saying *graphic novel* then. I knew the contents of the last page when I was sketching the first one. A 150 page graphic novel takes an inordinate amount of time to get done, which raises a difficulty. When I drew Page 1, I was still working at the factory, operating the guillotine to cut sheet metal interminably into rectangles to make ducting. By the end of Book 3, I was unemployed in Brighton with a wife and baby, and halfway through Book 4 was adrift in a distant tropic eating bananas. How does one stick to a plan through that? It was done, but I can feel the changes in point of view in the re-reading of it. It cannot be 'improved', needless to say, since I am now even further removed from any of those positions. They have become part of the story as has the quality of the drawing. An artist worth his salt is bound to be a different craftsman in 1980 at age 25 compared to 33 in 1988, not to mention that silver-haired geezer sitting down to edit the work in January 2000. Dates appear on most of the chapters, Acme Press removed them from their 1990 edition but I've put them back.

Many good things have been said about this book over the years. *The Comics Journal* included it in their hundred best of the century (at no. 51) while another critic in a history of the modern comic described it as "vivid, if amateurishly drawn". This presupposes that there was a consensus on how the true graphic novel should look, as early as 1980, when the great ones were neither yet made nor imagined. When the votes were in, "professional" did not rate in the criteria. Nevertheless, there was much that I felt needed retouching. How blissfully happy I would be if I came back to this work and found that all the pages were as good as Book 3 Page 1, Book 3 Pages 31-32, Book 4 Page 5 and that my occasional impatience and anxiety over ever getting it completed did not show as annoyingly as on Book 2 Page 35. I would start from scratch and redraw it all, I'd get rid of all that 'Alec' and 'Danny' stuff, but those who love me would not love to see me spend the rest of my life fixing the old when so much of the new remains to be done. I must content myself to do it briefly in my head, where it begins like this ...

"In 1977, Eddie Campbell was feeling that mental malaise that was to manifest itself in the wider sphere as punk. Having in his own mind condemned the world to wallow in its own stupidity and wearing an old jacket he picked up for a quid at Oxfam, he cheerfully worked his way down to the position of unskilled factory hand..."

BOOK ONE

A PINT OF BEER, A MEAT PIE AND THOU...

DANNY GREY NEVER REALLY FORGAVE HIMSELF

FOR LEAVING ALEC MacGARRY ASLEEP AT THE TURNPIKE.

Campbell 5/81

YOU'RE THE NEW MAN?

I DON'T FEEL LIKE ONE. NAME'S ALEC

DANNY

SUPPLIES

WORKS ENTRANCE

LANCER BOSS

LANCER

TRUND TRUND TR

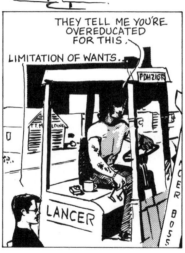

THEY TELL ME YOU'RE OVEREDUCATED FOR THIS.

LIMITATION OF WANTS..

PDH2IGR

LANCER

INDIFFERENCE TO THE UP AND THE DOWN. WHAT'S THE WORD? uh... greek philosopher...

PDH2IGR

LANCER

SOCRATES? PLATO?..XENOPHON.. ARISTOTLE...EURIPIDES...

stoical...

PDH2KB

LANCER

THAT'S NOT BAD YOURSELF.

I GOT THEM ALL FROM A SONG.

PDH2IGR

LANCER

RENE DESCARTES WAS A DRUNKEN FART..

PDH2GR

LANCER

I FIND IT A GOOD IDEA, WHEN DRINKING IN NEW COMPANY, TO NOTE DOWN SOME POSSIBLE CONVERSATION STARTERS BEFOREHAND.

SORT OF HELPS YOU OVER THE UNCOMFORTABLE PAUSES.

PREPARED NOTES, YOU MIGHT SAY.

shopping list, SHALL WE CHECK THEM OFF?

ACCORDING TO HIS BIOGRAPHER, JACK KEROUAC FELT THAT ONE OF THE MOST BEAUTIFUL IDEAS IN THE WORLD IS THE IDEA A CHILD HAS THAT HIS FATHER KNOWS EVERYTHING.

I PICKED UP THE WORD 'SYNCOPHANT' FROM MY FATHER. THE FIRST TIME I WENT INTO A PUB I CALLED THIS BLOKE A SYNCOPHANT.

" AND THE FELLOW REPLIED.. "uh.. YOU MEAN SYCOPHANT" OH NO, SAID I ... SYNCOPHANT

Then I looked it up.

WHAT ELSE HAVE YOU GOT THERE?

"MAN, IT HAS BEEN SAID, DIFFERS FROM OTHER ANIMALS IN ONLY TWO RESPECTS... HE DRINKS WHEN HE IS NOT THIRSTY AND HE MAKES LOVE ALL YEAR ROUND"

LIGHT 'N' BITTER AND BROWN 'N' BITTER, PLEASE.

GLOP

ANYWAY, AFTER THE DIVORCE I WENT TO GREECE. GOT WORK WITH A RESTAURANT THAT HAD ME SITTING ON THE BEACH ALL DAY BASHING SQUIDS ON A ROCK. IT WAS LIKE BEING BACK ON THE LINE AT FORDS.

GALOOP
GALOOP
GALOOP
GAL

LET'S TALK ABOUT THE WEATHER— YOU KNOW HOW WHEN IT RAINS ALL THE SNAILS CRAWL OUT OF THE GARDENS ONTO THE PAVE- MENTS AND YOU HAVE TO DO COMPLICATED BALLET-STEPS TO AVOID CRUSHING THEM.

yes, and

MY MOTHER'S IRISH. IN MY MOTOR- BIKE DAYS SHE ONCE SAID TO ME: "IF YOU FALL OFF THAT THING AND BREAK YOUR LEGS, DON'T COME RUNNING TO ME".

coincidence!! my mother too!

THE 'IRISH BULL'. IT'S CHARM LIES IN THE FACT THE SPEAKER IS UNAWARE IT DOESN'T MILK.

good way of putting it.

..TRYING TO EXPRESS THE NOCTURNAL NATURE OF CATS, SHE SAID THEY MUST BE NIGHT- BIRDS -

THAT GIRL OVER THERE... PLAYING DARTS. I FIND HER VERY ATTRACTIVE...

WHY?

oh no. you mean we... disagree.?

THIS ISN'T BEER SPEAKING.
I THOUGHT WE SAW THINGS THE
SAME WAY.
WHO SAYS WE DON'T.
YOU ARE OVERSENSITIVE!
YOU'RE THE BOOK-MAN!
I JUST WANTED YOU
TO PUT IT INTO WORDS
OK

ALEC MacGARRY LOOKED AT THE
GIRL AND HER BOYFRIEND AT
THE DARTBOARD. HE'D NEVER
SEEN THEM BEFORE. ON THE
FACE OF IT THEY WERE HOMELY
TYPES - THEIR CLOTHES LOOKED
SECOND-HAND.

AND SOMETIMES AFTER A LOT
OF BEER YOU CAN SEE THINGS
WITH A MYSTICAL CLARITY.
LIKE THE SHORTSIGHTED MAN
PUTTING ON GLASSES FOR THE
FIRST TIME. (ALEC WAS ALWAYS
GETTING ON THE WRONG BUS)

ALEC MacGARRY THOUGHT HE
COULD SEE ACROSS THE WORLD
AND HEAR BABIES SLEEPING.

SHE'S LIVING IN THE HERE AND
NOW. NO 'BUTS' OR 'IF ONLYS',
OR SAVE THE CASH IN CASE
SOMETHING BETTER COMES.
OF COURSE, I'M PROJECTING MY
OWN IDEALS
ONTO HER...
doesn't lessen
what you're saying

MAYBE SHE'S JUST IN LOVE.
SAME
RESULTS
- YES, YOU'RE RIGHT -
LIKE THE OLD SONG -
"THERE'S A SMILE ON MY
FACE FOR THE WHOLE
HUMAN RACE, WHY IT'S
ALMOST LIKE BEING IN LOVE"

ALEC MacGARRY NEVER FORGETS
THINGS SAID. WHEN HE WOKE
UP LATER THERE WAS A FINE
DRIZZLE ON HIS GLASSES.

DANNY GREY FORGETS MOST
THINGS. WHEN HE FOUND OUT
NEXT DAY HE'D LEFT MacGARRY
ASLEEP AT RETTENDON TURNPIKE
HE WAS SINCERELY APOLOGETIC.

THEY'D STOPPED TO SMELL
THE GRASS.

ALEC MacGARRY WALKED BACK INTO TOWN AND STOOD A LONG TIME IN FRONT OF A BUTCHER'S SHOP-WINDOW THINKING ABOUT THE POULTRY.

HE FELT NO INCLINATION TO GO HOME OR BACK THE WAY HE'D COME.

LONELINESS, HE REMEMBERED READING, IS NOT SO MUCH A LONGING FOR COMPANY AS A LONGING FOR KIND.

Josephine

E Campbell 6/81

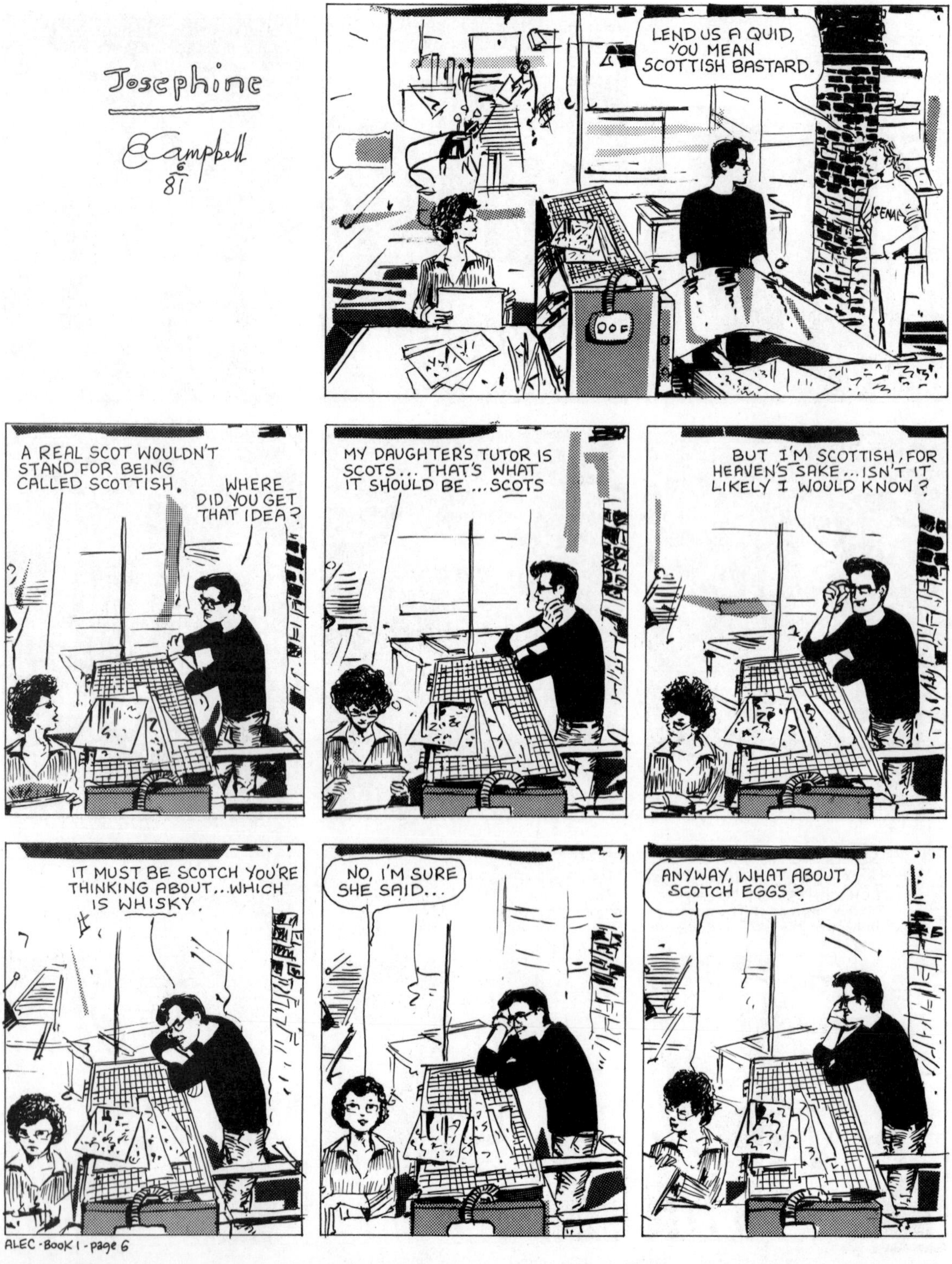

LEND US A QUID, YOU MEAN SCOTTISH BASTARD.
A REAL SCOT WOULDN'T STAND FOR BEING CALLED SCOTTISH.
WHERE DID YOU GET THAT IDEA?
MY DAUGHTER'S TUTOR IS SCOTS... THAT'S WHAT IT SHOULD BE ... SCOTS
BUT I'M SCOTTISH, FOR HEAVEN'S SAKE ... ISN'T IT LIKELY I WOULD KNOW?
IT MUST BE SCOTCH YOU'RE THINKING ABOUT... WHICH IS WHISKY.
NO, I'M SURE SHE SAID...
ANYWAY, WHAT ABOUT SCOTCH EGGS?

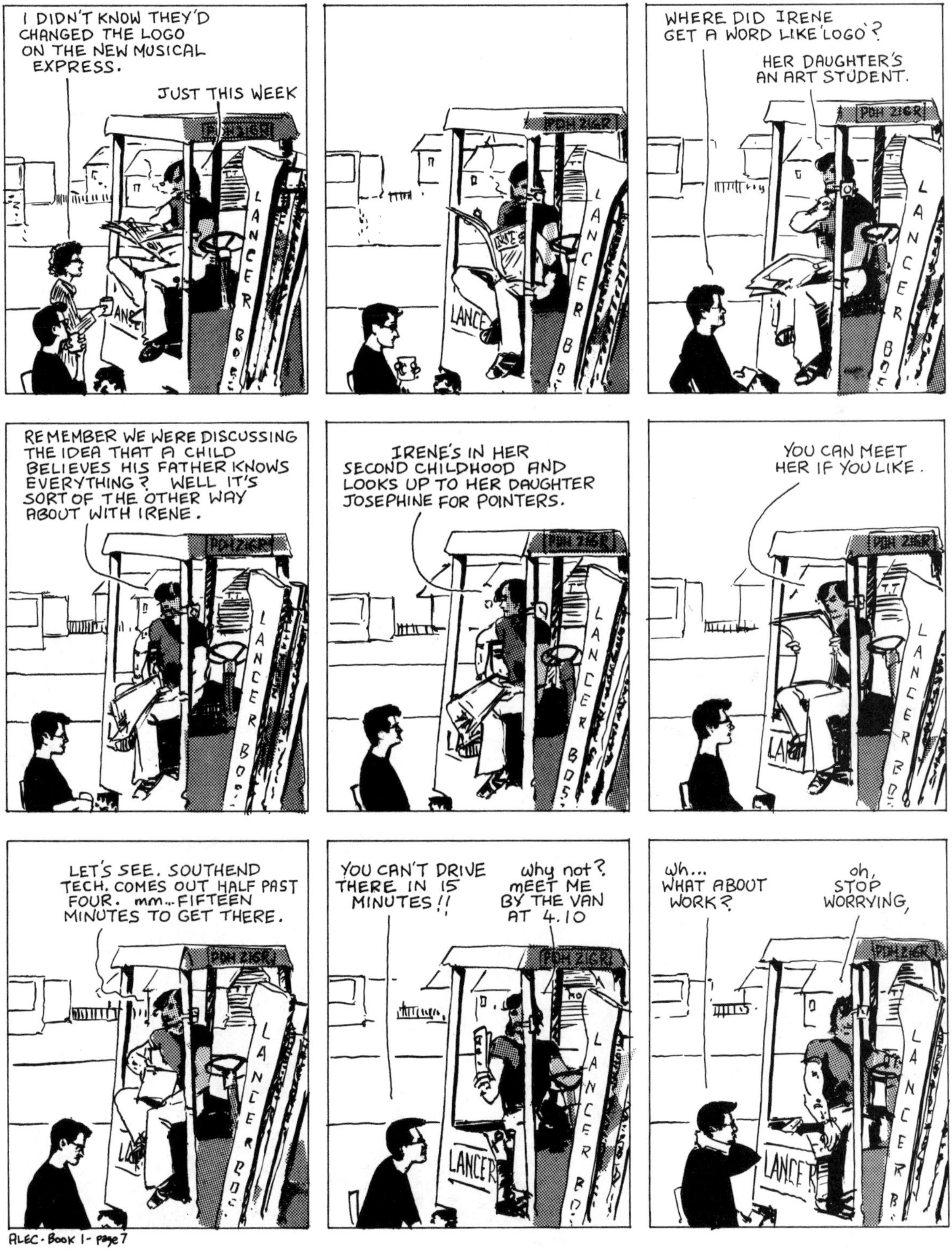
I DIDN'T KNOW THEY'D CHANGED THE LOGO ON THE NEW MUSICAL EXPRESS.
JUST THIS WEEK
WHERE DID IRENE GET A WORD LIKE 'LOGO'?
HER DAUGHTER'S AN ART STUDENT.
REMEMBER WE WERE DISCUSSING THE IDEA THAT A CHILD BELIEVES HIS FATHER KNOWS EVERYTHING? WELL IT'S SORT OF THE OTHER WAY ABOUT WITH IRENE.
IRENE'S IN HER SECOND CHILDHOOD AND LOOKS UP TO HER DAUGHTER JOSEPHINE FOR POINTERS.
YOU CAN MEET HER IF YOU LIKE.
LET'S SEE. SOUTHEND TECH. COMES OUT HALF PAST FOUR. mm... FIFTEEN MINUTES TO GET THERE.
YOU CAN'T DRIVE THERE IN 15 MINUTES!!
why not? meet me by the van at 4.10
wh... WHAT ABOUT WORK?
oh, STOP WORRYING,

ALEC MacGARRY DIDN'T GET TO MEET JOSEPHINE THAT DAY, AND MANY THINGS HAPPENED BETWEEN THEN AND NOW. BUT A FEW MONTHS LATER WHEN ALEC HAS A RENTED BEDSIT IN SOUTHEND DANNY GREY IS BRINGING JOSEPHINE ROUND FOR EVENINGS.

AND DO YOU KNOW...ALEC PAINTED THIS EIGHT YEARS AGO AT THE AGE OF FOURTEEN...

MacGARRY'S SELF-PORTRAIT OF VAN GOGH!

ARE YOU SURE IT WASN'T THE OTHER EAR HE CUT OFF?

NEVER GAVE IT A THOUGHT. mirror-image I suppose.

LET ME PUT THIS TO YOU AS A CONVERSATION-STARTER... DO YOU THINK JACKSON POLLOCK'S PAINTINGS CAN BE JUSTIFIED?

HE'S A DRIP.

YOU REALLY PUT THAT GUY ON A PEDESTAL.

DO YOU THINK SO?

I FIND HIM VERY HESITANT.. INDECISIVE... WHY'S HE WASTING HIS LIFE IN THAT FACTORY..?

IT SEEMED LIKE A GOOD IDEA, YOU BOTH BEING ARTISTIC. BUT YOU DIDN'T HIT IT OFF AT ALL.

ISN'T THAT LIKE EXPECTING DOGGIES TO GET ALONG BY DINT OF BEING MEMBERS OF THE UNIVERSAL FELLOWSHIP OF CANINES

YOU PUT THE DOGGIES TOGETHER AND THEY RIP THE SHIT OUT OF EACH OTHER

Point taken.

JOSEPHINE WOULDN'T THINK SO SHE TOLD ME OFF FOR SAYING 'DOGGIE'. SAID IT'S CHILDISH.

sounds Glaswegian to me.

BUT YOU KNOW. I REALLY FANCY HER. THOSE EYES.

WHAT YOU DON'T WANT ME TO SAY IS "THERE'S PLENTY MORE FISH IN THE SEA".

THAT'S GOOD...VERY UNDERSTANDING.. HEY! I'M IMPRESSED WITH THAT..

mmmm... HEY!!

ANYWAY, JOSEPHINE IS THE SORT WHO WILL GO PLACES, GET WHAT SHE WANTS.

YOU CAN SAY THAT AGAIN.

SHE GOT HOLD OF TWO TICKETS FOR BOB DYLAN'S BLACKBUSHE CONCERT.

you dawwg.

AND THAT I CAN'T RESIST.

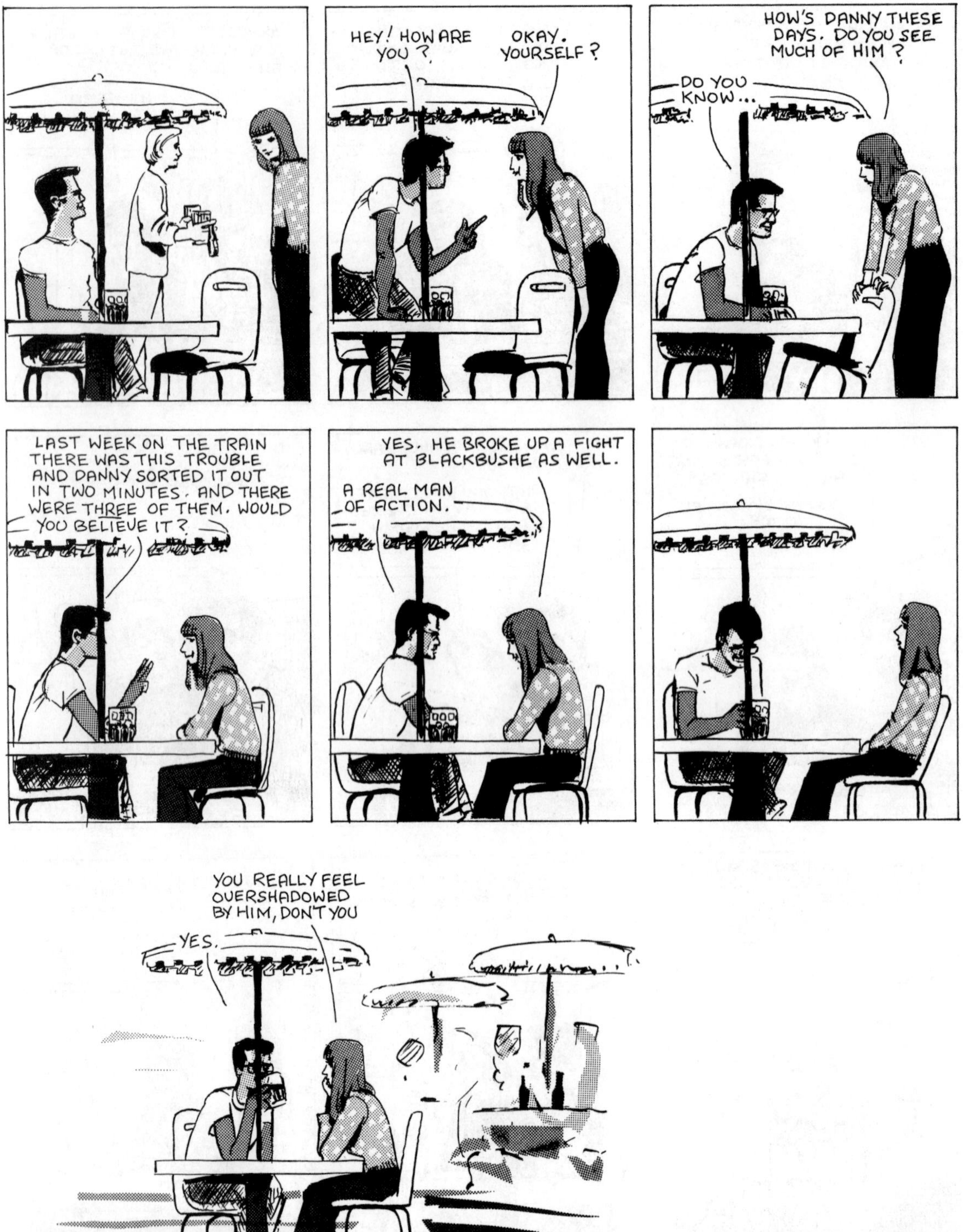
HEY! HOW ARE YOU ?
OKAY. YOURSELF ?
HOW'S DANNY THESE DAYS. DO YOU SEE MUCH OF HIM ?
DO YOU KNOW...
LAST WEEK ON THE TRAIN THERE WAS THIS TROUBLE AND DANNY SORTED IT OUT IN TWO MINUTES. AND THERE WERE THREE OF THEM. WOULD YOU BELIEVE IT ?
YES. HE BROKE UP A FIGHT AT BLACKBUSHE AS WELL.
A REAL MAN OF ACTION.
YOU REALLY FEEL OVERSHADOWED BY HIM, DON'T YOU
YES.

EAT: BEING SPECIAL OCCASION OF BIRTHDAY, MRS. MacGARRY SERVES UP RAINBOW TROUT WITH ALMONDS, THEIR EYEBALLS, FOR THE SAKE OF DELICACY, BEING REPLACED BY BRIGHT GREEN PEAS.

Eat, drink, be merry.

Campbell 7/81

FOR ALL WE KNOW IT COULD BE STANDARD ETIQUETTE—

I SUPPOSE SO

DID YOU HEAR THE ONE MUM CAME OUT WITH YESTERDAY?

TELL.

STOP TALKING ABOUT ME

DAD WAS AT A CHEESE AND WINE PARTY, AND WHEN HE WAS LATE HOME SHE SAID "I THINK YOU'VE BEEN DRINKING MORE THAN CHEESE AND WINE!"

DRINK: ALEC MacGARRY AND DANNY GREY MEET AT 6·30 SHARP, THE USUAL 'EARLY START' AND THEY SAMPLE THE ALE IN THE CASTLE.

THEN THE SWAN, THE QUART POT, RUNWELL HALL,

THE BELL, THE OASIS.

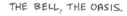

JIM BEAM $7

Haig

STELLA ARTOIS

AND ON OTHER OCCASIONS IN THE SHEPHERD AND DOG, THE COACH AND HORSES, THE KING'S HEAD, THE CROWN.

THE PRINCE OF WALES FEATHERS, THE CARPENTERS ARMS, THE BLUE BOAR, THE QUEEN'S HOTEL, THE HALF MOON, THE

RISING SUN, THE CHEQUERS, THE TRAVELLERS JOY, THE CHICHESTER ARMS... THE SPREADEAGLE.

WHERE THEY DRANK WATNEYS, TRUMANS, COURAGE, IND COOPE, GREENE KING, RIDLEYS, STONES, McEWANS, CHARRINGTONS, WILSON'S, JOHN SMITHS...

FROM MUGS AND GLASSES AND BOTTLES AND CANS.

THE KING CANUTE.. NOW THERE WAS A PUB.. BACK WHEN MARY WAS RUNNING IT. I REMEMBER ONE NIGHT WE SAT AT THE BAR DRINKING AFTER-HOURS.

AND MARY SAID SHE WAS GOING TO MAKE SOME BREAKFAST. I THOUGHT SHE WAS BEING SARCASTIC TO MAKE US GO HOME.

THEN SHE PULLED BACK THE CURTAINS AND THE SUN STREAMED IN.

SMOKE: ALEC MacGARRY PRODUCES HIS CONVERSATION PIECE FOR THE EVENING: TWO BROOMHANDLE CIGARS.

YOU HANDLE IT WELL FOR A NON-SMOKER, MATE.

ALEC BROUGHT THESE BACK FROM A BRIEF VISIT TO NEW YORK LAST YEAR, THIS YEAR BEING, IF YOU WILL TRANSPORT YOURSELF, PLEASE, 1977, AND HE TALKS AT GREAT LENGTH ABOUT IT.

DRINKING ICED TEA AND PLAYING TABLE TENNIS WITH PEGGY O'HARE IN HER BASEMENT RECREATION ROOM...

WALKING MY LAST NIGHT ALL THROUGH BROOKLYN TRYING TO MAKE IT LAST... I SMOKED A CIGAR SO CLOSE THAT I WATCHED THE SUNRISE WITH BIG RED LIPS.

PISS: MacGARRY URINATES WITH HEAD AGAINST THE WALL TO STEADY HIMSELF, NOT AN ADVISABLE PROCEDURE SINCE, IF THE FLOOR'S WET YOU MAY SLIP, CONSEQUENTLY BREAKING YOUR JAW ON THE URINAL.

AND BESIDES, PEOPLE HAVE BEEN KNOWN TO SMEAR SNOT ON THE WALLS.

TALK: GREY AND MacGARRY DISCUSS A KIND OF IDEAL SARTORIAL ELEGANCE, IN THEIR VIEW (FRIENDS BEING MERELY 'PEOPLE WHO BELIEVE THE SAME NONSENSE') YOUNG MENS' APPAREL OF SOME TWENTY YEARS PREVIOUS...

BOX JACKET

...NOT FROM A NOSTALGIC POINT OF VIEW, YOU WILL UNDERSTAND, THESE FELLOWS BEING A MERE 27 AND 22 YEARS RESPECTIVELY, BUT AESTHETICALLY SPEAKING, YESTERDAY'S ADONIS, AS IT WERE.

SLIM-JIM TIE

THE GREBE-TYPE, AS GREY EXPRESSES IT, AS IN GREATER-CRESTED GREBE, (REFERRING TO HAIRSTYLE) OR IN COMMON PARLANCE, THE TEDDY BOY.

..BUT NOT THE GAUDY TYPE OF TODAY

AS AN EXERCISE IN FLATTERY AND HUMAN STUDIES, DANNY GREY SINGLES OUT AN EX-GREBE TYPE FROM AMONG THE PATRONS OF THE PUBLIC HOUSE.

AND MOOCHES A LIFT.

SAFELY INSTALLED IN THE VEHICLE, DANNY GREY JOGS THE ORIGINAL GREBE-TYPE'S MEMORY WITH REGARD TO AN ARTICLE OF DRESS WORN IN CLASSICAL ANTIQUITY.

NATURALLY, THE FEMALE COMPANION IS NOT FLATTERED BY BEING TOO CLOSELY ASSOCIATED WITH FASHIONS THAT WALKED THE EARTH SO LONG AGO AND THE LADS ARE POLITELY LET OUT ONCE MORE AT THE TURNPIKE.

YOU MUST HAVE A FEW SLIM-JIM TIES AT HOME, MATE.

WHAT DO YOU MEAN?

WALK: DANNY GREY FEELS DEEPLY MORTIFIED. ALEC MacGARRY, EXHALED ONCE MORE INTO THE COLD NIGHT AIR FEELS INSTANT-ANEOUSLY EMBALMED...

...WHICH IS TO SAY, BIBULOUS, FUZZLED, AND TO BE HONEST, SENTIMENT NOTWITHSTANDING, SICK AS A DOG.

wait a minute

GENUFLECTING TO THE PATRON SAINTS OF NOVICE CIGAR SMOKERS, HE LOWERS HIS HEAD AND INTONES THEIR NAMES.

RUTH! HUGHIE!!

SLEEP: WHO KILLED SUNDAY?

THE REDEEMING FACTOR OF THIS SORT OF SITUATION IS THAT YOU NEVER KNOW WHERE YOU ARE (YOU KNOW THE FEELING)—EAR NOTES THAT IT IS SANDWICHED COSILY BETWEEN HEAD AND CUSHION, BRAIN DEDUCES YOU ARE HORIZONTAL AND THEREFORE IN BED— A BED. YOU SINK A LITTLE.—BODY HEAT RISES—.SOUR TASTE IN THE MOUTH.....the tail-end of your dream has just sneaked off....

EAT: ALEC'S BEEN USING THE COUCH AT DANNY'S GIRL-FRIEND VALERIE'S PLACE REGULARLY FOR A FEW WEEKENDS NOW. EVENTUALLY THERE ARE SIGNS OF LIFE FROM THE BEDROOMS, AND TALK OF BREAKFAST. PLAYING OF RECORDS. AND IN NO TIME AT ALL, THE SLIGHTEST MENTION OF DINNER.

The dating game:
me versus you.
E Campbell
8/81

DAVE BARNES, ON HIS WAY TO WORK, COMES UP BEHIND ALEC MacGARRY AND OBSERVES HIM CONVERSING WITH A YOUNG LADY WHOM WE SHALL CALL BETTY BOOP.

BARNES FANCIES THE GIRLIE, AND BY PROCESSES CONVOLUTED AND CUNNING THE TWO ARRIVE IN ALL SERIOUSNESS AT THE NOVEL PROPOSITION OF SWAPPING GIRL-FRIENDS

DAVE BARNES IS AT THIS TIME GOING OUT WITH JOSEPHINE PRINGLE WHOM ALEC MacGARRY HAS NOT YET MET AND TO WHOM HE MOST DEARLY DESIRES AN INTRODUCTION.

A WEEK LATER, IT COMES ABOUT LIKE THIS: MONDAY, SEPTEMBER 12, DAVE BARNES ASKS FOR A RAISE UNSUCCESSFULLY. HE PHONES FOR ANOTHER JOB AND LEAVES.

HE PROMISES TO CALL MacGARRY THAT NIGHT TO MAKE A DEFINITE PLAN. MacGARRY BUMPS INTO BOOP AGAIN ON HIS WAY HOME FROM WORK.

I HAD TO SEE YOU, ALEC. I'M GOING INTO HOSPITAL FOR A BIG OPERATION. I'VE MADE A WILL.

I'M LEAVING YOU SOME MONEY AS WELL AS THAT PHOTO THE PRIVATE DETECTIVE TOOK OF US WHEN I WAS LIVING WITH PETER.

MacGARRY AGREES TO MEET HER THE FOLLOWING NIGHT FOR A SYMPATHETIC DRINK AND PHONES BARNES TO MAKE THE NECCESSARY ARRANGEMENTS.

WHY'S JOSEPHINE GOING OUT WITH THAT NIT ANYWAY. YOU KNOW I HAD TO EVEN WRITE HIS QUIT-NOTICE FOR HIM.

IRENE PRINGLE ARRIVES AND PASSES ON A MESSAGE.

ALEC, DAVE SAID TO TELL YOU THE WHOLE THING'S OFF. HE SAID YOU'D KNOW WHAT THAT MEANS.

AND WHEN MacGARRY GETS HOME.

SOMEONE CALLED DAVE PHONED TO SAY HE'D PICK YOU UP AT SEVEN.

DAVE BARNES TURNS UP IN HIS FATHER'S DOGGIE-VAN (runs greyhounds) BUT INSTEAD OF JOSEPHINE HE BRINGS ADAM, WHO WORKS AT THE FACTORY.

BARNES DECIDES TO PICK UP JOSEPHINE ANYWAY, AND LEAVES MacGARRY IN RAYLEIGH TO RENDEZVOUS WITH BETTY BOOP.

THEY ALL MEET UP IN THE MIDDLE OF THE ROAD. THE FIRST TIME MacGARRY SEES JOSEPHINE SHE'S WEARING A JUNGLE HAT AS SHE'D MEANT TO STAY IN AND WASH HER HAIR.

oh dear.. WAS THIS MEANT TO BE A DOUB— I'VE FUCKED IT UP.

AFTER MUCH DRINKING, MacGARRY, JOSEPHINE AND ADAM ARE IN THE SAWDUST ON THE HOME ROUTE.

STOP TO COMPARE NOTES.

I GAVE HER MY PHONE-NUMBER- HOW ABOUT YOU?

DON'T WORRY ABOUT ME, MATE.

SHE SAYS SHE'S GOING INTO HOSPITAL FOR FOUR DAYS. WHY DON'T WE VISIT HER?

I DONNO... I DON'T THINK IT'S A GOOD IDEA.

DID YOU HAVE A GOOD TIME? POOR JOSEPHINE. I THINK DAVE WAS IGNORING HER BECAUSE OF THAT SILLY HAT.

BOOP'S GONE INTO HOSPITAL TODAY.

SERIOUS OPERATION?

YES

hmmm.

TELL ME ABOUT HER.

WELL, THERE WAS THE MARRIAGE WHICH WASN'T, THE PREGNANCY AND THE FALLING DOWN STAIRS, A PHOTO I'VE NEVER SEEN, AN UNCLE WITH A PRIVATE PLANE.

THURSDAY: DAVE BARNES' TWELVE YEAR OLD SISTER IS KILLED IN A RIDING ACCIDENT AT THE BOTTOM OF THE LANE.

ALEC MacGARRY AND DANNY GREY COME ACROSS JOSEPHINE (and the sweetest lady of this entire period, by name of Julia) — SHE DOESN'T KNOW THAT BAD NEWS.

FRIDAY: ADAM IS LAID OFF FROM THE FACTORY.

I DON'T CARE ABOUT THAT. IT'S MY GIRL-FRIEND SARAH GOING OFF WITH BARNES' MATE.

TUESDAY: BOOP CALLS ALEC.

OK, IF YOU SAY SO. LET'S SEE THE PHOTO THEN. THE NEIGHBOUR'S KIDDY MUST HAVE TAKEN IT?

yeah

SUNDAY: DAVE BARNES PICKS ALEC UP. AROUND TO HIS PLACE. SEEMS OKAY BUT AVOIDS THE SPOT WHERE HIS SISTER WAS FOUND. HIS FOLKS ARE AWAY AND HE'S REDECORATING THE HOUSE.

MacGARRY MEETS SARAH, WHO LIES SLEEPING, SITS SNOGGING AND IN THE PUB ASKS FOR A PIMMS No. 1. AND EATS THREE TOASTED SANDWICHES.

AND KEITH, WHO PAYS FOR ALL THE AFOREMENTIONED.

THEY ALL PILE INTO KEITH'S CAR AND GO TO PICK UP JOSEPHINE. BARNES INSTRUCTS HIM TO AVOID THE SPOT.

BARNES AND JOSEPHINE ARE IN THE BEDROOM. THE OTHER TWO ARE IN THE CAR. THE GIRL IN THE GROUND WILL NEVER KNOW THE JOYS OF COURTSHIP.

FRIDAY: BETTY BOOP CALLS ALEC. HE DATES HER UP WITH BARNES MUCH AGAINST HER TOKEN RATHERNOTS.

BARNES TAKES BOOP OUT ON SATURDAY, SUNDAY AND MONDAY.

FRIDAY: (THIS BY NOW OCTOBER 7) MacGARRY SEES BOOP IN THE STREET AND THEY'RE TALKING WHEN JOSEPHINE AND JULIA COME ALONG.

For God's sake don't say anything.

Reported overheard on bus:

I WONDER WHAT THAT DAVE'S PLAYING AT?

ALEC BOOK I · page 19

MONDAY: BOOP PHONES ALEC AND INFORMS HIM SHE HAD NOT CALLED DAVE ON SATURDAY, BUT HE'D COME ROUND ANYWAY AND APPEARS TO HAVE A CRUSH ON HER.

SHE TELLS HIM FURTHERMORE THAT DAVE BROUGHT WITH HIM A CHAP NAMED KEITH, AND SHE'D ATTEMPTED TO MATCH THIS CHAP WITH HER SISTER.

WEDNESDAY:
DAVE? - I THINK HE'S TRYING TO GIVE ME THE GENTLE SHOVE.

COME OUT WITH ME THEN

maybe.

THURSDAY: MacGARRY CHOOSES TO PLAY HARD-TO-GET AND TAKES A DIFFERENT ROUTE HOME FROM WORK.

JOSEPHINE PHONED DAVE LAST NIGHT BUT HE WASN'T IN. HIS MOTHER SAID HE WAS GOING OUT WITH BETTY BOOP. JOSEPHINE NATURALLY WAS VERY UPSET

yeah.

SARAH CAME ROUND CRYING, BUT FUCK 'ER. ALSO, YOU MUST HAVE HEARD DAVE CHUCKED BOOP AND HE'S GETTING ENGAGED TO THE BARMAID FROM THE JOLLY CRICKETER.

yeah.

BETTY BOOP PHONES —
SO I THOUGHT, DAVE AND MY MOTHER HAD THE SAME SURNAME AND BOTH ORIGINATE FROM HORNCHURCH, SO DAVE COULD BE THE SON OF THE SON OF THE BROTHER OF MY MOTHER'S FATHER. no, let me go back over that ...

JOSEPHINE ASKS IF YOU CAN LEND HER A RECORD, PLEASE, DANNY: 'SYMPATHY FOR THE DEVIL' BY THE ROLLING STONES.

LANCER

THE COMPANY VAN.
(using it to go out in the evening)
E. Campbell.
12/80   5/81

J. RODEN

RO
LIGHT
METAL
HAULAGE

HOLD ON, LOVE.
IT WON'T BE LONG.

HOW DO YOU FEEL?

broken leg...

HAS SOMEONE
CALLED AN
AMBULANCE?

YES

WILL SHE BE ALRIGHT?

I REALLY DON'T KNOW

YOU ARE A DOCTOR, AREN'T YOU?

NAH, I'M A FORKLIFT DRIVER.

SHOULDN'T YOU
KEEP AWAY?

DANNY GREY YANKS THE WHEEL AROUND WHILE STATIONARY.

SO WHEN HE REVERSES, THE WHEEL SPINS AND KNOCKS HIS THUMB OUT.

THE MANAGER SENDS HIM TO THE HOSPITAL TO GET IT CHECKED.

WHILE HE'S WAITING HE CAN'T HELP NOTICING THE OLD LADY. SHE'S BEEN WAITING A LONG TIME TO BE PICKED UP.

ARE YOU SURE YOUR DAUGHTERS COMING?

oh yes

MR. GREY, IT LOOKS LIKE JUST A BAD BRUISE

BUT YOU'VE BEEN HERE FORTY-FIVE MINUTES ALREADY

REST THE HAND FOR A DAY OR TWO AND YOU'LL BE FINE

MAYBE I CAN HELP. WHERE DOES SHE LIVE?

RAYLEIGH RD.

IS THAT IN EASTWOOD?

YES, I THINK IT IS

I'LL GIVE HER A LIFT, IF YOU LIKE.

WOULD YOU? THAT WOULD BE GREAT

WAIT HERE. I'LL BRING ROUND THE....uh... WAGON

HE PUTS ONE OF HER MITTS ON THE GRAB-HANDLE AND HELPS HER IN.

IT'S NEAR A CHURCH. YOU'RE A NICE BOY. ARE YOU MARRIED?

SHE KNOWS SHE LIVES IN RAYLEIGH ROAD BUT HASN'T A CLUE WHERE THAT IS. DANNY TRIES ASKING DIRECTIONS.

RAYLEIGH ROAD, MATE.

SORRY. NEVER HEARD OF IT.

HE WORKS HIS WAY AROUND CHALKWELL PARK WHERE HE SPIES SOMEONE HE KNOWS.

SORRY, DANNY. CAN'T HELP YOU.

IT'S TIME FOR A TEA-BREAK.

IT'S MANY A YEAR SINCE A HANDSOME FELLOW TOOK ME OUT TO TEA. DID YOU SAY YOU WERE MARRIED?

I'VE BEEN TRYING TO GET YOU HOME FOR AN HOUR. HAVE YOU NO IDEA AT ALL WHERE YOU LIVE?

THERE'S ONLY ONE THING FOR IT: DANNY GRABS HER HANDBAG.

SQUAWK.

THE PENSION BOOK IS IN THERE.

RAYLEIGH ROAD, LEIGH! SHOULD HAVE DONE THIS IN THE FIRST PLACE.

LEIGH POLICE STATION:

THERE IT IS. NOT FAR. IF YOU CAN'T SORT IT OUT, COME BACK AND LEAVE HER WITH US.

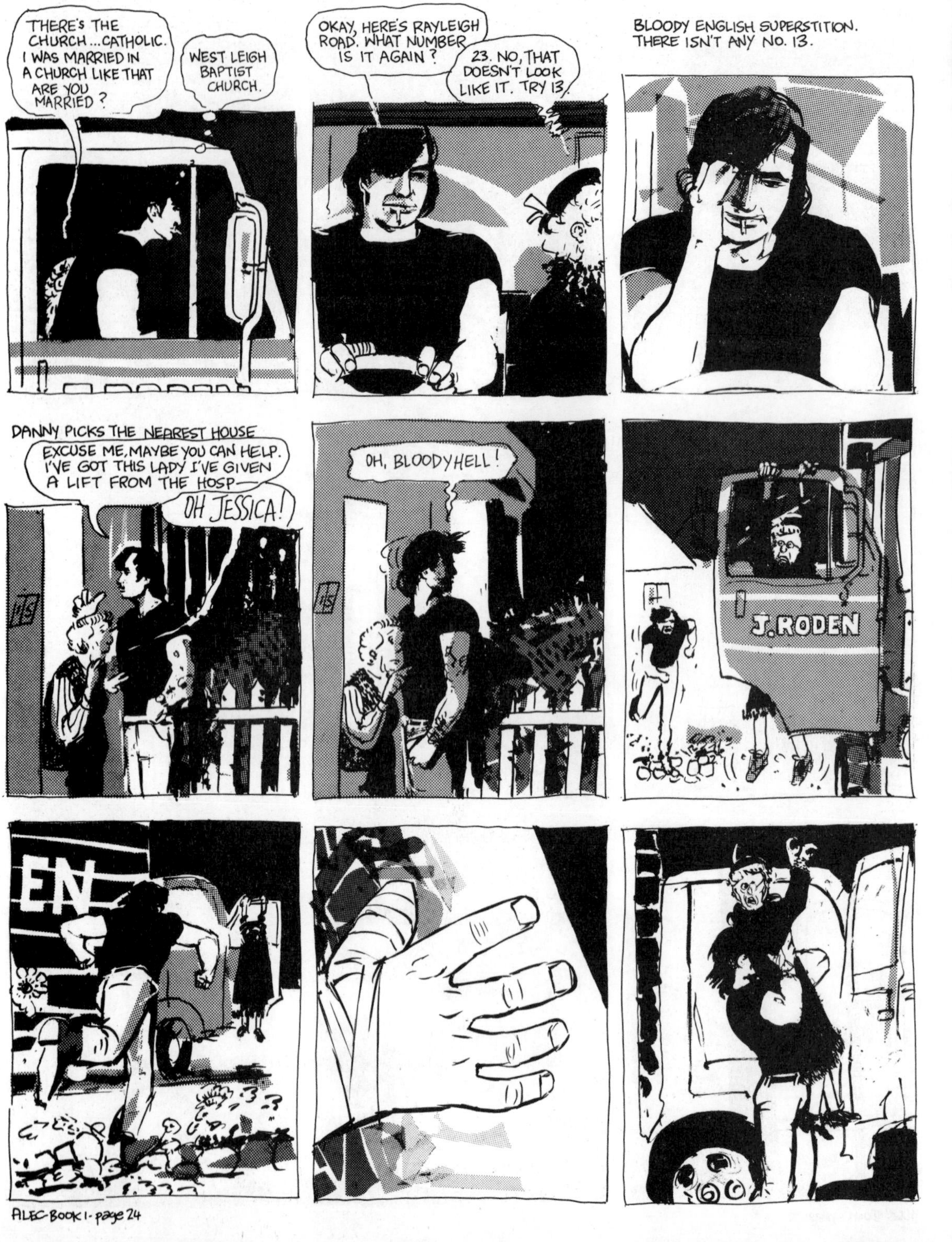
THERE'S THE CHURCH ...CATHOLIC. I WAS MARRIED IN A CHURCH LIKE THAT ARE YOU MARRIED ?
WEST LEIGH BAPTIST CHURCH.
OKAY, HERE'S RAYLEIGH ROAD. WHAT NUMBER IS IT AGAIN ?
23. NO, THAT DOESN'T LOOK LIKE IT. TRY 13.
BLOODY ENGLISH SUPERSTITION. THERE ISN'T ANY NO. 13.
DANNY PICKS THE NEAREST HOUSE
EXCUSE ME, MAYBE YOU CAN HELP. I'VE GOT THIS LADY I'VE GIVEN A LIFT FROM THE HOSP—
OH JESSICA!
OH, BLOODYHELL!
J. RODEN
EN

NINETY-FOUR YEARS OLD, ALEC. THAT'S WHAT BOWLED ME OVER.

THE COMPANY VAN CERTAINLY OPENS THE DOOR TO ADVENTURE

YOU CAN SAY THAT AGAIN.

AND THEY'RE SENDING ME FURTHER AFIELD ON DELIVERIES I'M GOING ALL THE WAY UP TO GLASGOW TOMORROW. SPARE SEAT IF YOU WANT TO COME

A TRIP HOME. NOW THAT'S TEMPTING.

ALEC MacGARRY, OF COURSE, WORRIES ABOUT WHAT WILL BE SAID WHEN HE GET'S BACK TO WORK THREE DAYS LATER.

YOU COULD ALWAYS PHONE IN SICK

FROM THE MOTORWAY ?

AH YES, THE OPEN ROAD...

ALEC MacGARRY IS A MAMMOTH IN THE ICE.

ECampbell 9/81

SEND A REFUGEE-AIRLIFT OR
THE VALKYRIE OR SOMETHING

UM..YEP

BOTTLEOPEN HIM.

(THE EMOTIONAL PARALYSIS GOES LATER— NOT THE POUNDING HEAD)

HOW CAN I LOOK HIM STRAIGHT IN THE EYE AGAIN ?

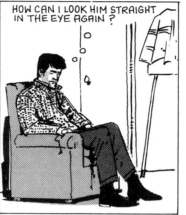

DANNY GREY HAD SET UP A DOUBLE DATE WITH GIRLS HE KNEW FROM THE OLD KING CANUTE DAYS..

AND ALEC MacGARRY HAD PLAYED IT JUST AS YOU WOULD LIKE, EXCEPT FOR ICING UP AT THE CRUCIAL LAST MINUTE.

INTO THE BARGAIN DANNY HAD HIRED A CAR FOR THE WHOLE BUSINESS —

DAMN HIM ANYWAY— WHAT'S HE EXPECT ME TO BE ?, —

SORRY ABOUT SATURDAY NIGHT—...

SORRY WHY? NO NEED, MATE !

..TOO MUCH VODKA, I GUESS —

DRINKING IN BILLERICAY—

I JUST DON'T FEEL AT HOME IN THE WORLD —

I ENVY THE EASE WITH WHICH OTHER PEOPLE MAKE USE OF THE AMENITIES, BY WHICH I MEAN.. EVERYTHING FROM...SEX TO PLAYING A JUKEBOX.

I THINK YOU'RE ONE OF COLIN WILSON'S 'OUTSIDERS'- HAVE YOU READ THAT BOOK?

no –

ah!- ONE YOU HAVEN'T READ.

I IDENTIFIED WITH THAT BOOK MYSELF.. mm.. A FRIEND OF MINE ONCE SAID TO ME.. "YOU KNOW WHAT I LIKE ABOUT YOU, DANNY? YOU'RE A WASTER."

yes.. fits.

THE REASON FOR BEING IN BILLERICAY WAS THAT DANNY HAD USED THE COMPANY VAN TO TRANSPORT A PUNK ROCK GROUP TO THIS GIG –

ON THE HOME ROUTE ALEC MacGARRY PUTS ON A SPONTANEOUS DEMONSTRATION (OF CONFIDENCE)

YOU'RE NO' PUTTIN' HER IN THE BACK WI' THE JUNK ARE YE?!

?

is he coming too?

?

HIS PATTER IS FLUENT.

HIS WORDS COME OUT LIKE MAGICIANS' DOVES.

AND IT IS ALL, YOU UNDERSTAND OF COURSE, BY WAY OF MAKIN' UP.

ALEC SHORTLY OBSERVED THAT SOCIAL SKILL AND SEXUAL SKILL ARE NOT UNRELATED — (RE-ENTER BETTY BOOP)

I WANT YOU TO COME TO PARIS WITH ME FOR A WEEKEND —

THERE WON'T BE ANY FUNNY BUSINESS, I HOPE...

umm.. YOU MEAN SEX?

NO, OF COURSE NOT, SILLY — I MEAN YOU WON'T TRY TO SWOP ME AGAIN...

:hmmph:

PARIS — in short —

.. flights promptly began calling Roissy tower, *Hullo Charlie! Hullo Airport Charlie!* ...They received in reply the austere mouthful, *This is Roissy-Charles De Gaulle Airport*

Official spokesmen explained smoothly that "use of the abbreviation 'C for Charlie' is natural as it is part of the international alphabet". But pilots were strictly forbidden to repeat this lèse-majesté in future in case 'Charlie' should be confused with 'Orly'."

staying in Rue de la Republique It's cold for January — See you next week —

Betty

BOOK TWO

still-life with fried egg 21/6/83.

LOVE AND BOTTLES

WHEN ALEC MacGARRY'S FOLKS MOVED BACK UP NORTH HE DECIDED TO STAY IN THE AREA AND QUICKLY FOUND A BEDSIT ON WESTCLIFF SEAFRONT.

Campbell 10/81

(SAME WEEKEND AS THE DAFT JANUARY FLIGHT TO PARIS I MENTIONED BEFORE) THE LAND-LADY HAD ADVERTISED FOR A BUSINESSMAN TYPE AND WASN'T TOO SURE ABOUT MacG AT FIRST.

THE PREVIOUS TENANT HAD APPARENTLY DONE A BUNK, AMONG OTHER THINGS, BECAUSE ALEC MET ALL HIS NEW NEIGHBOURS AT ONCE OF A SATURDAY MORNING...

...WHEN ALL TEN BELLS IN THE HOUSE WERE RUNG BY A POLICE-MAN AND THE POSTMAN (WITH MacGARRY'S NEW POSTOFFICE ACCOUNT BOOK— ALL OF TWENTY QUID IN IT)

A LAUREL AND HARDY SCENE WHICH INTRODUCED ONLY ONE CHARACTER OF NOTE; MALCOLM, A POET OF SORTS.

— ANYTHING FOR SIMPKINS?

...STANDING CONFUSED IN THE DOORWAY LOOKING LIKE NOEL COWARD OR SOMETHING,

(AND NEXT DAY MOST OF THE TENANTS GOT OUT AND PUT THEIR NAMES UNDER THEIR BELLS).

SOME WARM JUNE NIGHTS YOU UNCORK THE BOTTLE AND THE SITUATIONS TUMBLE OUT BACKFLIPPING AFTER EACH OTHER LIKE CIRCUS MIDGETS

ALEC MacGARRY WANDERS INTO A CERTAIN PUB AND ORDERS A PINT.

REALIZING AFTER A MINUTE THAT HE HAS INADVERTENTLY COME IN SOUTHEND'S GAY HAUNT HE BECOMES SWIFTLY INTOXICATED BY THE NOVELTY OF THE SITUATION (AND THE BARMAID)

WOULD YOU LIKE THIS STOOL?

NO THANKS. A GENTLEMAN ALWAYS TAKES THE WEIGHT ON HIS ELBOWS.

HEH HAH

oh you

WHAT ARE YOU DRINKING?

THAT'S VERY GOOD OF YOU. ORANGE JUICE.

"SET 'EM UP JOE"

ARE YOU DOING ANYTHING AFTERWARDS?

maybe.

WHAT DO YOU WANT ME FOR MY BODY OR MY MENTALITY?

MY DEAR, YOU ARE THE PERFECT COMPOSITE!

(AND OTHER SUCH WORD-GAMES)—IT TURNS OUT THAT MacGARRY AND THE LITTLE GAY FELLOW GET QUITE COSY AND AT EVENING'S-END...

GOOD LUCK WITH THE BARMAID.—

AND YOU WITH THE BIG GERMAN GUY.—

MacGARRY MAKES A DATE WITH THE BARMAID.

CAMBRIDGE ROAD

AND BRIMMING OVER WITH *JOIE DE VIVRE*, GOES JOGGING NEXT MORNING WITH FRIEND MALCOLM FROM UPSTAIRS.

AS FOR THE DATE, ALEC HANDLES IT ALL WRONG, AND MAYBE IT WOULD HAVE BEEN FINE IF HE LEFT IT THERE, BUT HE HAS TO GO BACK AND TRY TO START OVER

um...

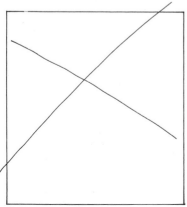

FEELING EMBARRASSED AND SILLY, HE GETS OUT OF TOWN FOR A FEW DAYS, MOOCHING A LIFT UP TO GLASGOW WITH ONE OF THE COMPANY'S DELIVERIES.

ODEN
ETAL SUPPLIES

GREAT IRRITATION THROUGH HAVING PUT ON THE WRONG PAIR OF GLASSES, ONE OF THOSE AGRESSIVELY UGLY STATEMENTS YOU OBTAIN WHEN YOU PREFER THAT THE WORLD JUST DOESN'T LIKE YOU.

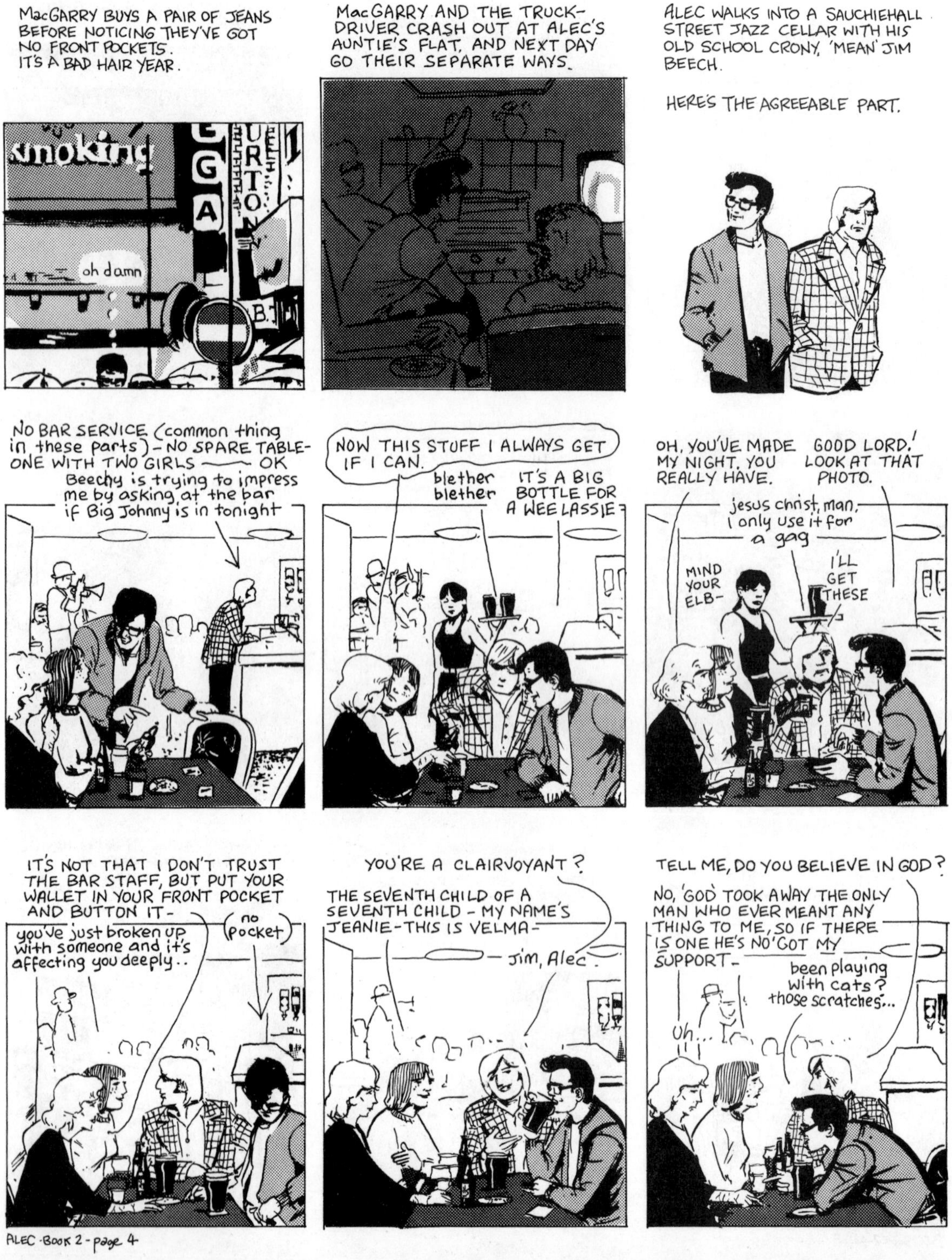
MacGARRY BUYS A PAIR OF JEANS BEFORE NOTICING THEY'VE GOT NO FRONT POCKETS.
IT'S A BAD HAIR YEAR.
smoking
oh damn
MacGARRY AND THE TRUCK-DRIVER CRASH OUT AT ALEC'S AUNTIE'S FLAT, AND NEXT DAY GO THEIR SEPARATE WAYS.
ALEC WALKS INTO A SAUCHIEHALL STREET JAZZ CELLAR WITH HIS OLD SCHOOL CRONY, 'MEAN' JIM BEECH.
HERE'S THE AGREEABLE PART.
NO BAR SERVICE (common thing in these parts) - NO SPARE TABLE-
ONE WITH TWO GIRLS —— OK
Beechy is trying to impress me by asking at the bar if Big Johnny is in tonight
NOW THIS STUFF I ALWAYS GET IF I CAN.
blether blether
IT'S A BIG BOTTLE FOR A WEE LASSIE
OH, YOU'VE MADE MY NIGHT, YOU REALLY HAVE.
GOOD LORD! LOOK AT THAT PHOTO.
jesus christ, man, I only use it for a gag
MIND YOUR ELB-
I'LL GET THESE
IT'S NOT THAT I DON'T TRUST THE BAR STAFF, BUT PUT YOUR WALLET IN YOUR FRONT POCKET AND BUTTON IT-
(no pocket)
you've just broken up with someone and it's affecting you deeply..
YOU'RE A CLAIRVOYANT?
THE SEVENTH CHILD OF A SEVENTH CHILD - MY NAME'S JEANIE - THIS IS VELMA-
Jim, Alec.
TELL ME, DO YOU BELIEVE IN GOD?
NO, 'GOD' TOOK AWAY THE ONLY MAN WHO EVER MEANT ANY THING TO ME, SO IF THERE IS ONE HE'S NO'GOT MY SUPPORT-
been playing with cats? those scratches...
Oh...

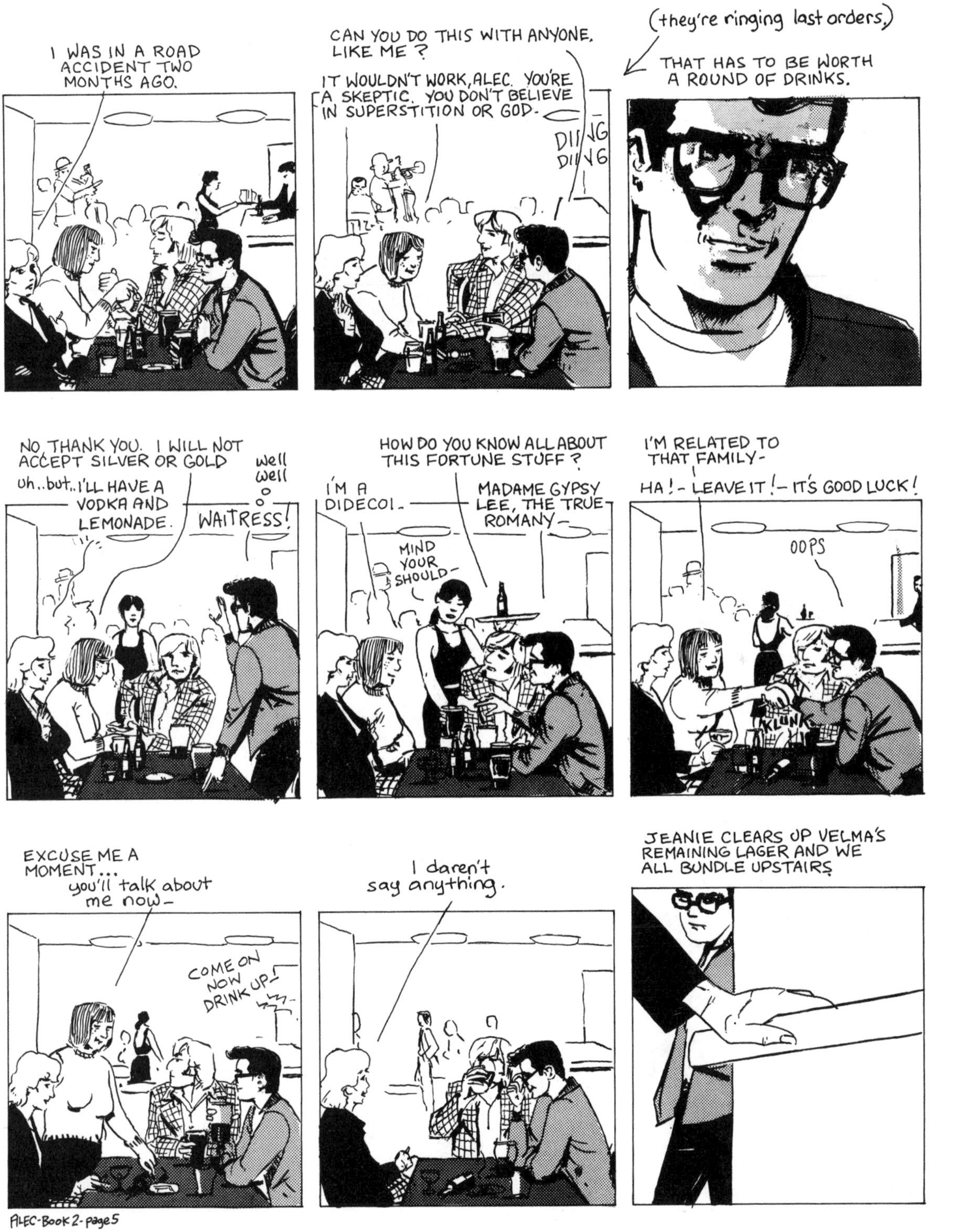
I WAS IN A ROAD ACCIDENT TWO MONTHS AGO.
CAN YOU DO THIS WITH ANYONE. LIKE ME ?
IT WOULDN'T WORK, ALEC. YOU'RE A SKEPTIC. YOU DON'T BELIEVE IN SUPERSTITION OR GOD-
DING DING
(they're ringing last orders,)
THAT HAS TO BE WORTH A ROUND OF DRINKS.
NO, THANK YOU. I WILL NOT ACCEPT SILVER OR GOLD
uh..but.. I'LL HAVE A VODKA AND LEMONADE.
well well
WAITRESS!
HOW DO YOU KNOW ALL ABOUT THIS FORTUNE STUFF ?
I'M A DIDECOI-
MADAME GYPSY LEE, THE TRUE ROMANY-
MIND YOUR SHOULD-
I'M RELATED TO THAT FAMILY-
HA ! - LEAVE IT ! - IT'S GOOD LUCK !
OOPS
KLUNK
EXCUSE ME A MOMENT...
you'll talk about me now-
COME ON NOW DRINK UP-
I daren't say anything.
JEANIE CLEARS UP VELMA'S REMAINING LAGER AND WE ALL BUNDLE UPSTAIRS

DOWN SAUCHIEHALL STREET GUYS ARE BUSTLING OUT OF SIDE-STREET BARS IN USUAL GLASGOW STYLE. VELMA SHUDDERS AND HER COMPOSURE RUNS OFF LIKE A NEST OF DISTURBED SPIDERS.

THAT SOUNDS OVERDRAMATIC, BUT THAT'S THE WAY IT SOMETIMES COMES AT YOU WHEN YOU'VE HAD A SNOUTFUL . AND LITTLE MYSTERIES WORK YOUR MIND. ABOUT THE SCRATCHES, I MEAN.

WELL, LOOK—I'VE GOT TO GET BACK TO THE HOSTEL—IT'S BEEN...NICE . SEE YOU AROUND-JIM, ALEC. SEE YOU LATER, VELMA.

OK, JAMES. VELMA'S WITH ME.

(this is not the big possessive act, but in case of any beef over who pays what — Beechy professes to be the meanest guy in Glasgow)

(BEECHY TAKES US BY THE SCENIC ROUTE)

YOU DON'T HAVE A GLASGOW ACCENT— COUNTRY?

I WAS BORN IN PARTICK-BUT MOVED WHEN I WAS EIGHT-TO ALLOA . HOW ABOUT YOU, ALEC?

: ALEC :

WHEN A GIRL OF YOUR FANCY REMEMBERS YOUR NAME IT'S MUSIC.

BUT THE ACCENT —— mm — NOT GLASGOW, LIKE SPITTING OUT PLAYING CARDS, OR ROLLED SOUTHEND VOWELS (GARLIC)

TRANSLUCENT— A (RAINDROP IN THE) LAKE .

AND HALF-POUNDER. SALAD AND ALL THE TRIMMINGS.

MY FRIEND, JIM BEECH, HERE...

...CAME INTO THIS RESTAURANT WITH A JEWISH ACQUAINTANCE OF HIS AND JIM OFFERED TO PAY THE BILL. THE NEXT DAY'S HEADLINE READ:- *JEWISH VENTRILOQUIST FOUND MURDERED*

HEE HEE

SO WE ALL TELL A JOKE BEECHY TELLS ONE ABOUT CONDOMS. MacGARRY KICKS HIM UNDER THE TABLE.

IT'S MY TURN.

THERE WAS THIS BEAR- GALLUMPHING THROUGH THE FOREST— *gallumph* *gallumph* *gallumph*

MacGARRY IS GALLUMPHED ON SOME UNIVERSAL MATERNAL LAP.

THEN HE SPOILS IT.

DOES THIS JOKE HAVE A RABBIT IN IT?

oh you've heard it before...

THE KIDDY WHO KNOWS THE STORY BUT WANTS THE GALLUMPHING BIT ALL OVER AGAIN.

WHAT'S THE NEXT MOVE? SEE HER HOME? AND DO THE BUSINESS? AT SOME PREARRANGED SPOT A GUY JUMPS OUT FROM BEHIND A WALL AND HITS YOU WI' A BOTTLE? DON'T ASK ME.

WHERE'S VELMA?

GONE TO PHONE HER LANDLORD AND TELL HIM TO LEAVE THE DOOR OPEN.

CANCEL ALL PREVIOUS PLANS AND I'LL SEE YOU IN A FEW DAYS?

NO, I DON'T THINK SHE'LL BE BACK   reckon?

I can't figure her out at all - she didn't even eat her salad.

BEECHY KICKS UP A FUSS ABOUT THE BILL— CLAIMS THERE WAS NO SALAD DRESSING AND GETS A FEW PENNIES KNOCKED OFF (BUT DOESN'T QUESTION SPLITTING THE BILL HALF AND HALF) — (PAL OF MINE) —

WE WAKE UP NEXT MORNING IN BEECHY'S BED —

JAMES!? HAVE YOU GOT SOMEONE IN THERE?

Groannn...

THAT NIGHT WE HAVE A DRINK IN BURNSIDE AND GO OVER THE WHOLE THING, WHEN IN WALKS A FELLOW CALLED 'NED' KELLY, WITH HIS WIFE AND A CAMERA —

I NEED A COUPLE OF GUYS FOR SOME PHOTIES —

BEECH AND MacGARRY PRETEND TO LIKE SOME AWFUL WOMEN FOR THE SAKE OF A FEW PICTURES.

mum didn't bring me up to be no gigolo —

AND AFTERWARDS SOMEONE DRIVES KELLY AND HIS MRS. BACK TO THEIR ROOM IN POLLOCKSHAWS (MAYBE IT WAS KELLY HIMSELF. I'M LONG PAST REMEMBERING)

AND MacGARRY HAS A COFFEE THERE —

WELL, I'M OFF.. REMEMBER TO SEND ME A PHOTO —

SURE —

HE DIDN'T, OF COURSE, BUT THAT'S HOW IT GOES —

WE'RE ONLY PASSING THROUGH . . . . .

THE KING CANUTE SITS WELL OFF THE BEATEN TRACK
YOU NEED A CAR — E Campbell 12/81

THE KING CANUTE HAS ALREADY
ACQUIRED MYTHICAL STATUS IN THE
HEAD OF ALEC MacGARRY THROUGH
THE STORIES OF DANNY GREY.
A VISIT IS INEVITABLE

DANNY GREY'S OLD PAL, JOHN
GODFREY IS THE CONNECTING
LINK.

JOHN GODFREY LIVED WITH HIS
WIFE AND HER DAUGHTER DOWN
ON WESTCLIFF SEAFRONT

JOHN GODFREY'S SISTER-IN-LAW,
AN INTRIGUING FIGURE MENTIONED
HERE AND THERE USED TO OWN
THIS OLD DOOMED MINI-VAN
TILL JOHN TOOK IT OFF
HER HANDS.

JOHN'S GIVING ALEC A LIFT FOR A
WHILE TO THE PICK-UP-POINT
WHERE HE GETS ANOTHER LIFT.
ITS MORE A SOCIABLE THING
THAN A PRACTICAL NEED

THESE PEOPLE SLEEP WELL
SOMETIMES ALEC HAS TO
GO INTO THEIR BEDROOM
AND WAKE THEM UP.

HEY!

JOHN MOVES HIS FAMILY INTO
A CARAVAN ON HIS PARENTS'
PROPERTY NEAR THE KING CANUTE
DANNY HELPS HIM SHIFT STUFF.

GOT YOUR PRIORITIES
RIGHT, MATE.?

JEN SAID PAMELA WANTED TO
WATCH THE TELEVISION—

MMF

I DON'T REALLY WANT TO WATCH IT—MUM JUST THOUGHT I'D LIKE TO

oh fuck it

THE KING CANUTE SITS ALONGSIDE THE RIVER AT THE END OF A THREE-MILE NO-THROUGH COUNTRY ROAD. IT'S NOT A PLACE YOU'D PASS BY ACCIDENT, EXCEPT ON A BOAT.

EVERYBODY'S WHO'S THERE PLANNED IT.

WHICH NOW INCLUDES US.

THE KING CANUTE

NOBODY CAN JUST GO IN THIS
PLACE FOR A QUIET DRINK.
FIRST NIGHT I'M HERE THERE'S
A RUCKUS OUTSIDE AT
CLOSING TIME.

THE POLICE ARE ARRESTING
RICHIE ON A COMPLAINT NOBODY
CAN EVER FIGURE OUT.

SOME PERSONAL BEEF
BETWEEN HIM AND A PAL.

WHILE BIG JIM BATEMAN'S ORGANISING EVERYONE, THE LANDLADY'S SAINT
BERNARD'S IN RICHIE'S CAR AND NO-ONE CAN GET HER OUT. IT'S A BLACK AND
WHITE *VENTORA* WITH AN EAGLE PAINTED ON THE BONNET SO YOU'D
THINK IT COULD FLY. NOW DANNY'S GOING TO TEAR OFF IN IT AND
GET RICHIE OUT OF THE JUG. HE'S GOING TO STORM THE
HALLS OF LAW AND ORDER

WE'RE TRYING TO FIND LIFE'S
NARRATIVE THREAD AND LOOKING
FOR IT IN THE WRONG MOVIES

DON'T LET DANNY DO ANYTHING SILLY, ALEC—

I'LL WATCH HIM. (ME, ALEC MacGARRY WHO THINKS THIS IS HILARIOUS)

NYW 578G

WE'RE TEARING ABOUT IN THE NIGHT LIKE STARSKY AND HUTCH IN BROKEN DOWN OLD CARS

I TOLD YOU IT'S A WANKER, THAT MOTOR—

HOW DOES THE BONNET OPEN? IT DOESN'T.

WHAT THE HELL'S HE DONE TO IT?

INSTEAD WE SHOULD BE SERENADING YOUNG LADIES ON BALCONIES

LIKE PENNY MOORE FOR INSTANCE, JOHN GODFREY'S SISTER-IN-LAW

MEDIUM T.........

SHE'S NOW DRIVING A WOLSELEY 1300 WITH A BOOT FULL OF COLD CHINESE TAKEAWAY FROM AN EARLIER PARTY.

HER OLD MINI-VAN BREAKS AN AXLE AND JOHN HAS TO ABANDON IT.

MUCH LATER WE SEE IT IN THE PAPERS

Shock of van used in glue sniffing peril

RESIDENTS in a South Woodford council estate have been shocked to discover a glue-sniffing den in a decaying van in a corner of their car park.

Neighbours have seen young people in and around the van and chased them away in the past.

"I thought they were just youngsters who'd found a quiet place for a kiss and a cuddle together," said one man whose flat overlooks the car park where the van has been left. "I looked inside the van and was horrified at what I saw."

Plastic

The van contains dozens of used plastic bags and eight or so glue tins used in the practice of glue sniffing.

Police have been called to the scene several times and

ANOTHER FLOOR.

GOD SAVE THE KING.

GOD SAVE THE COW.

ANOTHER JAPE

ANOTHER FLOOR

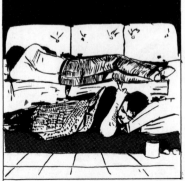

GOD BRING HOME THE BACON

...GOING BY TRAIN ACROSS GERMANY. I WAS IN A COMPARTMENT WITH SEVERAL TURKISH BUSINESSMEN.

IT WASN'T A SLEEPING COMPARTMENT. I WAS TRYING TO SLEEP UPRIGHT IN MY COAT AND THE TURKS... AFTER A BIG SPREAD WHICH THEY ATE WITH VICIOUS LONG KNIVES...

...ALL GOT UP AND CHANGED INTO PYJAMAS.

THE MAN WHO GIVES ME A LIFT TO WORK FROM CHALKWELL PARK EVERY MORNING... TOM HIS NAME IS. HE FORGOT TO TELL ME HE WAS HAVING MONDAY OFF...

SO ON MONDAY I WALKED ROUND TO HIS PLACE JUST THE SAME...

TOM WAS TOO POLITE TO MENTION THAT HE'D ARRANGED TO STAY HOME. SO HE PUT ON HIS WORK-CLOTHES AND DROVE ME THE TEN MILES.

come on, Tom— we're late

I DIDN'T GIVE IT A THOUGHT TILL THE AFTERNOON WHEN I REALIZED THERE WAS NO LIFT HOME.

CHRISTMAS DAY AT BIG JIM BATEMAN'S HOUSE. GOD BLESS THE TURKEY. BOXING DAY AT VALERIE'S

POOR LITTLE VALERIE, I ALWAYS HAD A DEEP SYMPATHY FOR HER. TWICE MARRIED, NEARLY THREE EXCEPT DANNY DROPPED OUT AT THE LAST MINUTE. ONLY TWO MONTHS AGO.

I WENT ROUND WHILE SHE WAS AT WORK TO PICK UP MY CLOTHES. SHE HAD A NEW BLUE DRESS IN THE WARDROBE ... for her big day.

I ALMOST STAYED JUST ON THE STRENGTH OF IT.

BUT YOU MUSTN'T THINK I'M INSENSITIVE. CALLOUS, YES BUT NEVER INSENSITIVE.

THIS SOUNDED LIKE SPLITTING HAIRS TO ME, LIKE OTHER DISCUSSIONS WE'D HAD.

"IMPRESSIONISM" IS WHERE YOU PAINT WHAT'S IN YOUR HEAD AS OPPOSED TO WHAT YOU SEE

no, no, no.

INSIST ON DEFINING IT THAT WAY IF YOU LIKE, BUT YOU'RE IN DANGER OF LOSING AN IDEA, WHICH IS MORE IMPORTANT THAN A WORD; THE CAPTURING IN PAINT OF EFFECTS OF LIGHT, AIR, TIME OF DAY.

BUT I SEE WHAT HE MEANT— AFTER ALL, HE WAS SENSITIVE TO ALL MY OWN ANXIETIES IN A WAY.

I'VE BEEN THROUGH IT MYSELF, MATE.

LANCET
LANCET BOS

AT THE SAME TIME, AND THIS IS WHAT IMPRESSED ME MOST, HE HAD AN INTRINSIC GRASP OF JUNGLE-TYPE CONFRONTATIONS. (AT THE PREVIOUS YEAR'S WORKS XMAS PARTY.)

OUTSIDE, ALEC!!

What's up?

BETTY SAYS YOU TOLD HER TO BE WARY OF ME —

(DANNY SAID I SHOULD HAVE KNOWN BETTER, WHICH STRIKES ME NOW AS A PRETTY FAIR OBSERVATION) —

DAVE, YOU SHOULD BELIEVE NONE OF WHAT YOU HEAR AND HALF OF WHAT YOU SEE —

AND SMILING VALERIE TURNS UP BEHIND THE BAR AT GATOR'S, THE NEW DISCO. EVERYONE TURNS UP AGAIN SOONER OR LATER.

LIKE JOSEPHINE PRINGLE SENDING CRYPTIC MESSAGES THROUGH HER MOTHER.

...ASKED ME TO ASK IF YOU CAN REMEMBER THE TITLE OF THE FILM LED ZEPPELIN MADE.

sorry, can't stop now, Irene —

KEN- YOU'RE A LED ZEPPELIN NUT - WHAT WAS THE FILM THEY MADE?

'THE SONG REMAINS THE SAME —'

— hhmm —

ARSENAL

ONCE WHEN HE LET HER DOWN.

JOSEPHINE WOULD LIKE TO BORROW THE 10cc ALBUM 'HOW DARE YOU'

LANCER

THE NICEST THING IN THIS LIFE IS JUST TO BE WITH YOUR FRIENDS. NO BIG STORY NEED COME OF IT. THE ADRENALIN MAY NOT FLOW.

REN

BUT THOSE THINGS ARE NECESSARY TOO. ENERGY BUILDS UP AND YOU BECOME RESTLESS IN THAT FINE COMPANY AND IT'S TIME TO GO.

GO BOOMERANGING ACROSS THE COUNTRY AND GET IT OUT OF YOUR SYSTEM.

PREST

THERE'S AN EXPRESSION DANNY USES SOMETIMES, WHICH HE GOT FROM HIS FATHER, WARTIME R.A.F. MAN.

"THE MEN CAN'T WAIT TO GET ASHORE AND GET SOME DIRTY WATER OFF THEIR CHESTS"

GIRLS. I HAD AN ON-OFF THING WITH A TALL BLONDE GIRL THAT DIDN'T HAVE MANY DAYS AS PLEASANT AS THIS CHRISTMAS.

I'D VISIT ONE NIGHT A LARGE LADY NAMED PAM, WITH TWO BOTTLES OF WINE, AND HAVE ALL THE PAINT SCRAPED OFF MY BACK.

...KISS HER GOODBYE IN THE MORNING LIKE SHE'S MY WIFEY AND GO TO WORK OBLIVIOUS OF THE RAIN -

...GET LITTLE LEAPS OF PLEASURE EVERY TIME I BUMP INTO HER AGAIN... BUY HER A DRINK.

YEAH, I'LL AMOUNT TO SOMETHING -

I'M SHARPENING MY CLAWS -

NEW YEAR'S EVE MY BROTHER AND I ARE STUCK 30 MILES NORTH OF BIRMINGHAM HEADED BACK TO LONDON WHEN THE SNOW STARTS

WE COME ACROSS THE STRAND
LIKE A LOG ON A DUCK-POND...

E Campbell 9/82

WE, THAT IS, ALEC MacGARRY AND
BRENDAN MacGARRY ON HAZARDOUS
RETURN TRIP FROM CHRISTMAS
VISIT TO THE FOLKS IN BLACKPOOL
— ARE STRANDED IN LAMBETH
FOR HOGMANAY.

AND MEANWHILE THE BIG SCENE
AT THE KING CANUTE HAS ALREADY
STARTED.

BLACK ICE ~ Four Wickford men die in car that goes off road on A130 and finishes upside down in water-filled ditch.

CAR BURSTS INTO FLAMES ~ on Pitsea flyover causing pile-up of twenty-five cars and two coaches

POLICE MAN ~ breaks pelvis and youth breaks back jumping 30 ft. from flyover to avoid skidding car – eighteen other people treated in hospital – A13 closed for 6 hours.

TANKER AND LORRY DRIVERS STRIKE ~ and at the works we run out of heating fuel – getting some through later but in the meantime they decide to pipe diesel fuel into the heating tank, diesel at 90p gal. costing three times as much.

SNOWED UNDER ~ the weather comes out in sympathy with the striking railmen and council workers today ~.

COMING HOME FROM WORK ONE NIGHT, ALEC MacGARRY GETTING LIFT FROM TOM AND FALLING ASLEEP IN THE FRONT SEAT...

...COMES AWAKE TO FIND TOM HAS GOT CAUGHT IN DRIFT AND ASKED BUNCH OF PASSERS-BY TO HELP PUSH THE CAR...

...BUT TOO POLITE TO WAKE UP MacGARRY.

ONE NIGHT AT THE KING CANUTE—

THIS IS THE WINTER OF MY DISCONTENT—..AS THE CHAP SAID — SHOULDN'T THAT BE OUR DISCONTENT?

uh—

I THINK YOU'LL FIND IT'S THE ROYAL 'WE'— RICHARD III SPEAKING THEREFORE 'OUR' DISCONTENT—

I SAY!—ARE YOU A FELLOW THESPIAN?

WHAT STRATA ARE YOU IN?

ACTUALLY I'M A FORKLIFT DRIVER

ONE SWEET NIGHT IN JANUARY DANNY GREY COMES IN THE MINERVA WITH LITTLE PENNY MOORE.

WHO GIVES ME A PERSONAL BIG SMILE

AFTERWARDS TAKES DANNY TO WHERE SHE STABLES HER HORSE—

BEST NOT GO TOO NEAR—HE DOESN'T LIKE PEOPLE MUCH—

THEN OTHER GIRLS OCCUPIED HIS TIME AND I THOUGHT MORE AND MORE ABOUT PENNY. ONCE DRIVING TO SOUTHEND FROM THE CANUTE HE REMARKS THAT A LITTLE GIRL WE'VE JUST PASSED LOOKS LIKE PENNY'S DAUGHTER.

I DIDN'T KNOW SHE HAS ONE, DIDN'T SEE, ASK WHAT SHE'S LIKE AND SO ON.

IN MARCH IT'S PENNY'S BIRTHDAY PARTY AND SHE TELLS HER SISTER JEN TO BRING DANNY ALONG... 'AND HIS FRIEND ALEC'.

PLEASED TO HAVE BEEN REMEMBERED AND DECIDE I WILL MAKE SOME KIND OF PLAY FOR PENNY TONIGHT.

PARTY'S OFF, MATE.

WHAT'S UP THEN?

SOME BLACK ICE ON ASHINGDON HILL, APPARENTLY. SHE HIT THE FRONT OF A LORRY AND THEY SAY THE CAR'S A WRITE-OFF.

JOHN SAID SHE LOOKED QUITE BASHED ABOUT. LOST A COUPLE OF TEETH...

ALL ABOUT THE FIGHT AT GATOR'S, THE NIGHT-SPOT WHOSE GIMMICK IS A LIVE ALLIGATOR IN A GLASS ENCLOSURE. IT NEVER BATS AN EYE.

Eddie Campbell 10/3/83.

ALEC MacGARRY AND DANNY GREY ARE THERE WITH SMIFFY AND A GUY THEY CALL THE VIKING.

MONICA'S THERE. HER BOYFRIEND'S IN AUSTRALIA FOR THREE MONTHS AND SHE'S HOBNOBBING WITH DANNY MEANWHILE.

MONICA'S ON THE DANCEFLOOR PINCHING ARSES.

SHE DRINKS LAGER LIKE A SQUIRREL WITH A NUT.

STEPHANIE'S THERE TOO. THE GIRLS ARE DOING IMPRESSIONS OF TV COMEDIANS WHEN THE PUNCH-UP STARTS.

YOU AIN'T APOLOGISED FOR TALKING TO MY WIFE LAST WEEK

I DON'T REMEMBER MEETING YOUR WIFE? IS SHE -- ? UH--

THIS WOULD BE A NON-INCIDENT EXCEPT THAT AT THE FIRST HINT OF AGGRAVATION A NUT DROOLING LIKE PAVLOV'S DOG RUSHES UP.

FROM MacGARRY'S POINT OF VIEW A GLIMPSE OF WHITE SHIRT AT THREE O'CLOCK.

LEAVE THAT ONE TO DANNY.

DON'T TAKE EYES OFF THIS ONE.

DANNY GREY STEAMS IN.

THE CLUB BOUNCER TRIES TO NIP IT IN THE BUD.

AS DANNY GOES DOWN HE SEES MacGARRY STILL BENDING AN EAR.

SMIFFY PINS A HEAD TO THE GROUND. THE ALLIGATOR'S SEEN IT ALL BEFORE.

STAY!

THE VIKING IS CORALLING THE GIRLS AROUND THE CORNER OF THE BAR.

WHILE THE BOUNCER THREATENS MacGARRY'S AMIGOS WITH THE BIG HEAVE, PAVLOV'S DOG THROWS A RABID FIT IN THE BACKGROUND.

IT ENDS WITH THIS RIPPED-SHIRT WHIRLIGIG — TRUE.

WHEN YOU TELL AND RETELL A STORY YOU TEND TO STREAMLINE IT, GIVE IT A DRAMATIC SHAPE — LEAVE OUT NICE LITTLE TOUCHES LIKE MY PAL PAM WAITING TO NOBBLE THE NEXT WHITE SHIRT THAT COMES UP —

ME, FULL OF REMORSE 'CAUSE EVERYONE'S FIGHTING MY FIGHT AND I DON'T ACTUALLY HIT ANYONE.

BLESS ALL MY FRIENDS.

KISS THEM GOODNIGHT AT THE STATION.

ABSENTMINDEDLY WALK IN THE PARCELS ROOM.

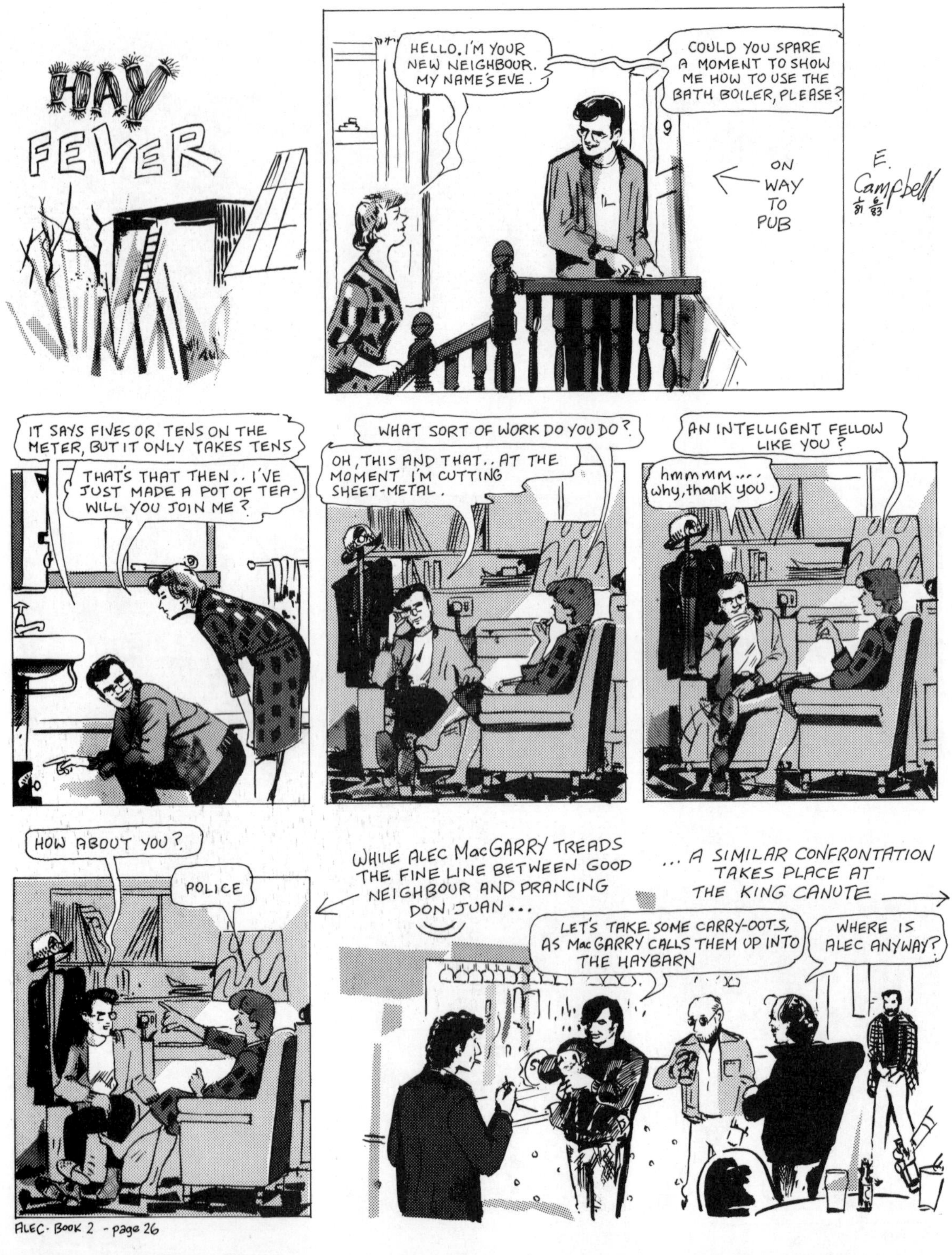

HAY FEVER
HELLO. I'M YOUR NEW NEIGHBOUR. MY NAME'S EVE.
COULD YOU SPARE A MOMENT TO SHOW ME HOW TO USE THE BATH BOILER, PLEASE?
ON WAY TO PUB
E. Campbell 1/81 6/83
IT SAYS FIVES OR TENS ON THE METER, BUT IT ONLY TAKES TENS
THAT'S THAT THEN.. I'VE JUST MADE A POT OF TEA - WILL YOU JOIN ME?
WHAT SORT OF WORK DO YOU DO?
OH, THIS AND THAT.. AT THE MOMENT I'M CUTTING SHEET-METAL.
AN INTELLIGENT FELLOW LIKE YOU?
hmmmm.... why, thank you.
HOW ABOUT YOU?
POLICE
WHILE ALEC MacGARRY TREADS THE FINE LINE BETWEEN GOOD NEIGHBOUR AND PRANCING DON JUAN...
... A SIMILAR CONFRONTATION TAKES PLACE AT THE KING CANUTE
LET'S TAKE SOME CARRY-OOTS, AS MacGARRY CALLS THEM UP INTO THE HAYBARN
WHERE IS ALEC ANYWAY?

THE CASE OF THE GREAT HAY ROBBERY —

AFTER ABOUT AN HOUR UP THERE DANNY GREY REALIZES HE MUST HAVE DROPPED HIS WATCH AND STARTS LOOKING FOR IT

NEIGHBOURING MRS. WILLIAMS BLOWS THE WHISTLE

THE GENDARMES ARRIVE IN DUE COURSE

ALL RIGHT! WE KNOW YOU'RE UP THERE - WE KNOW THERE WERE FOUR OF YOU!!

SMIFFY IS ARRESTED IN JAMES CAGNEY FASHION

HAHA! HE ONLY TRIED TO OUTRUN THE ESSEX SPRINT CHAMPION!

IF YOU'RE GOING TO LOCK ME UP ALL NIGHT YOU'LL HAVE TO GET IN TOUCH WITH MY WIFE - SHE'S NOT ON THE PHONE.., MY NAME'S JOHN GODFREY,. the caravan etc.

EMPTY POCKETS!

sigh..I WONDER IF THEY'LL LET US OUT ON BALE...

SHUT UP AND GO TO SLEEP!

HA HA HA HA

NEXT DOOR

I COULD UNLOAD A CRAP BUT I DON'T FANCY SNIFFING IT ALL NIGHT.., GUESS I BETTER HOLD ON TO IT.., THERE WAS THIS BLOKE IN MY CLASS AT SCHOOL USED TO HOLD ON TO IT—

TOM THE TURD THEY CALLED 'IM.

.. HE'D GO TO THE TOILET ONCE A FORTNIGHT AND IT WOULD COME OUT TWO FEET LONG.., THE FRONT END WOULD CURL AROUND THE U-BEND AND THE BACK END WOULD STICK OUT OF THE WATER LIKE BEACHY HEAD LIGHTHOUSE..

THEY ALWAYS HAD TO GET THE JANITOR IN TO BREAK IT UP WITH A SHOVEL—

DO YOU KNOW THE ____

A SOUTHEND PUB

NOT REALLY

WELL WE WENT UP THERE AND SEARCHED ALL THE PROSTITUTES FOR THE $300

SOUNDS LIKE A HORRID PLACE.. I WONDER IF STEGGY STILL DRINKS IN THERE

JOHN GODFREY'S
GOOD LADY WIFE
GETS THE NEWS

MORNINK, MATE-WHAT YOU IN FOR?

KICKIN' HAYSTACKS!

MOVE ALONG

A WEEK LATER EVERYONE
IS STILL TALKING ABOUT IT—

ALL THAT STRAW... WITH A COUPLE OF ANIMALS MY FRONT PORCH WOULD HAVE LOOKED LIKE A NATIVITY PLAY!

WHAT WE'LL NEED IS A CHARACTER WITNESS..

I'D LIKE TO-BUT I'M IN COURT MYSELF NEXT WEEK FOR HOLDING THE ST. VALENTINE'S DISCO WITHOUT A LICENCE -

HEY, YOU'LL NEVER BELIEVE IT! WHILE I WAS DRINKING TEA WITH YOU LAST WEEK ALL MY FRIENDS GOT ARRESTED ON A HAYSTACK! ISN'T THAT HILARIOUS!

THEY SHOULDN'T HAVE BEEN THERE .

THE FARMER WITHDRAWS ALL
COMPLAINTS - BUT THE POLICE
PUSH THE CASE THROUGH ANYWAY.

JAMES SMITH, GEORGE WAITE, JOHN GODFREY, AND DANIEL GREY.. WOULD YOU STAND IN THAT ORDER PLEASE... .

DANNY SAVES A BON MOT FOR THE SUM-UP

AS FOR MRS WILLIAMS.. IN THE WORDS OF AN AMERICAN COMEDIAN.. THEY COULD HAVE USED HER AT PEARL HARBOUR .

THEY WERE FINED TWELVE QUID EACH FOR DAMAGES AND COURT COSTS

THE VAN IS STILL FULL OF STRAW
FROM THE FIASCO. SEVERAL NIGHTS
LATER, IN THE WEE HOURS:

BRRRRR - FUCK THE HOMOSEXUALITY - WE'LL HAVE TO GET CLOSER-

I WATCHED THE WHOLE THING FROM THE PUBLIC GALLERY AND AFTERWARDS JOHN GODFREY DROPPED ME OFF HOME —

I STAND AROUND AWHILE AND THINK TO MYSELF —— GREAT FOOLISH DOINGS AT THE KING CANUTE...

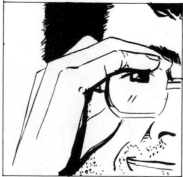

ON THE BANK OF THE RIVER CROUCH WHICH KING CANUTE CROSSED NEARLY A THOUSAND YEARS AGO TO FIGHT THE BATTLE OF ASHINGDON —

HUNDREDS OF GUYS SWARMED ABOUT IN THE OCTOBER MUD HITTING EACH OTHER WITH

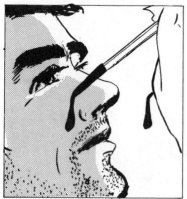

KNIVES AND AXES AND ENGLAND HAD A DANISH KING FOR A WHILE

SOMEBODY CAME OUT OF THE PUB ONE AFTERNOON WITH A METAL DETECTOR —

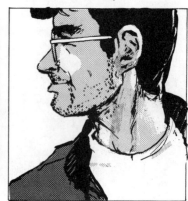

AND SAID TO AN OLD FARMER WASN'T THERE A BATTLE HERE

AROUND ABOUT TEN SIXTEEN AND THE FARMER SAID WELL

I BEEN HERE ALL MORNIN AN I AIN'T SEEN NO BATTLE

E.Campbell

The
Great
Waster
ⓒ
E Campbell
12 5
81 83

DANNY GREY, GREAT WASTER
AND MENTOR TO ALEC MacGARRY,
ORDERS MORE BEERS

ALEC MacGARRY, LESSER WASTER,
SOMEHOW LOCKS HIMSELF IN A
SLEEPING BAG AT JOHN GODFREY'S
CARAVAN ONE NIGHT.

We'll have you out
of there in
no time

THE 'WASTING' PHILOSOPHY GETS
EXPOUNDED MORE FULLY ANOTHER
NIGHT AFTER 'MORE BEERS' DOWN
THE TRAIN-LINE IN BRENTWOOD.

MacGARRY GETS THAT OVERSENSITIVE
FEELING YOU GET WHEN THINGS
ARE VEERING OUT OF WHACK, LIKE
SOMEONE'S SANDPAPERED THE
SOLES OF YOUR FEET.

REGARDING THE NOBLE ART OF
WASTING, ITS ALL VERY FINE
AND DANDY TO SIT AT HOME
STARING AT THE BEDROOM
WALL...

...BUT ONE MUST BE SEEN TO BE
WASTING...IT MUST BE A PUBLIC SQUAN-
DERING OF GOOD TIME AND MONEY.

LET'S DRAW UP A
MANIFESTO !!

Put this in it
for starters:

"A POOR LIFE THIS, IF FULL OF CARE,
WE HAVE NO TIME TO STAND AND STARE"

W.H.DAVIES.
(whoever
he is)

NOW, PICTURE;...YOU'RE GOING
ACROSS FRANCE...THE CONTIN-
ENTALS ARE MOVING UP AND
DOWN THE CORRIDOR... A
LADY IN BLACK'S TAPPING
ON THE WINDOW.

MacGARRY IS STILL WAITING FOR THE PUNCH LINE—

THAT WAS THE INTER-CITY GOING PAST ABOUT 12 INCHES AWAY—

EARLIER, DANNY HAD BEEN DOING ONE OF HIS 'INTERVIEWS' TO GET THE INSIDE TRACK ON BRENTWOOD CLUBS, PRETENDING TO BE SOMEONE ELSE.

IF DANNY HAD SCRAGGED HIMSELF, ALEC PICTURES HIMSELF IN HIS DEVOTION KEEPING UP THE PRETENSE.

AT THE KING CANUTE THERE'S AN ENDLESS ROUND OF CELEBRATION.
ONE NIGHT IT'S DANNY GREY'S BIRTHDAY, WITH GEORGE WAITE
SINGING FOOTBALL TERRACE CLASSICS

NEXT NIGHT IT'S SOMEBODY ELSE'S.

Well, what do you SING on John Wilkes Booth's birthday?

ONE OF THOSE NIGHTS PENNY MOORE
WALKS IN, HER FACE STILL HURT
FROM THE CAR CRASH.

AND ALEC CAN'T QUITE QUITE CATCH
HER ATTENTION ATTENTION

THEY WANT TO HIDE DANNY'S TRUCK
KEYS BUT ALEC CAN'T SEE IT FITTING
IN WITH HIS SOCIAL SCHEDULE.

hmm...HE'S DETERMINED TO
DO A DELIVERY TOMORROW
SO HE CAN GET UP TO
GATOR'S ON MONDAY—

RODEN

DANNY GREY'S ABILITY TO GO WITHOUT FOOD FOR GREAT LENGTHS OF TIME IS CONSIDERED SIGNIFICANT. THIS IS HIS FIRST BITE IN THE 30 HOURS ALEC'S BEEN WITH HIM

THE PREVIOUS WAS YESTERDAY A.M. ON A KENT DELIVERY WITH BIRTHDAY CAKE COURTESY IRENE PRINGLE. HE SPIED CHILDREN FEEDING SWANS AND IMPROVISED A PARTY.

MacGARRY'S FLAT—

HEY, IF YOU'RE STAYING, HAVE THE BED—

4 A.M. STAGGERING ABOUT—

HE'D LEFT THE HEADLIGHTS ON SO I HAVE TO PUSH THAT DAMN BIG THING—AND BEING SUNDAY HAVE TO LOOK FOR FOOD IN THE KOSHER SHOPS—

BACK AT THE KING CANUTE, LOUISE, THE LANDLADY, HAS HER FRIENDS HANG AROUND LATE FOR A DRINK. GREY GETS A BIT MIFFED WITH MacGARRY FOR CHUCKING A SLEEPING BAG.

AND LOUISE WITH EVERYONE FOR BACKFLIPPING OUT OF THE CHAIRS—

COME NOW, DARLINGS—YOU'LL RUIN THE FURNITURE

THEN WE'RE DOWN BY THE RIVER-WALL... GODFREY'S GONE HOME BUT LEFT US WITH HIS BONGO—MONICA SLIPS AND SQUEALS AND MacGARRY KICKS IT OVER—

AND IN THE OLD SILENT GLOOM THAT RICKETYCLACK MUST GO RIGHT BACK TO THE CARAVAN OH DEAR....

FROM SLEEPING BY THE RIVER, NEAR THE PUB, DANNY ADVANCES TO SLEEPING IN THE ESTABLISHMENT ITSELF, A FEAT CONFERRING ENORMOUS PRESTIGE UPON HIM. HE'S ALREADY IN THE BAR WHEN THE REGULARS START ARRIVING ON EASTER SUNDAY MORNING.

I CAN DO SOME BACON AND SAUSAGE FOR BREAKFAST, DARLINGS, BUT I'M AFRAID THERE AREN'T ANY EGGS —

WHAT? NO EGG SARNIES?!

AN EGG FOR THE PIANO-PLAYER! I SHALL GO OUT AND COME BACK WITH AN EGG.

AS IT HAPPENS, A PLATOON OF AIR-TRAINING CADETS ARE ENCAMPED ON GROUND ATTACHED TO THE PUB, MAINLY DUE TO THE HEAD MAN BEING AN UNCLE OF LOUISE'S —

now where on Easter Sunday? Excuse me. Any idea where I can buy some eggs, mate?

CERTAINLY — GO AND SEE THE PROVISIONS TENT — TELL THEM MR. GLENN SENT YOU — WE HAVE TO GET RID OF ALL PERISHABLE STOCK AS WE'RE GOING HOME TODAY, AND SINCE IT'S ALL GOVERNMENT ISSUE I CAN'T CHARGE YOU FOR IT —

SO DANNY COMES BACK WITH 18 EGGS AND LOUISE COOKS A BIG BREAKFAST

AND WHILE THEY'RE WAITING GEORGE PLAYS 'FUR ELIZE' IN THE STYLE OF CHICO MARX.

FOR ELSIE

ANY REMAINING DOUBT ABOUT DANNY GREY BEING AN AGENT SENT BY THE GODS IS REMOVED FROM ALEC MacGARRY'S NOODLE...

WHEN HE SEES THE DOVE DROP OUT OF NOWHERE AND SIT ON DANNY GREY'S SHOULDER AND WHISPER INSTRUCTIONS IN HIS EAR.

I SAW MY AIMLESSNESS SUMMED UP ONE MORNING IN THE KING CANUTE WHEN GEORGE WAITE LEFT HIS CLOGS BY THE COAL FIRE, WENT TO THE PIANO AND PLONKED OUT 'KNEES UP MOTHER BROWN' IN THE STYLE OF WAGNER...

ECampbell
7/83

I'D JUST SPENT THE EASTER WEEKEND WITH MY FOLKS IN BLACKPOOL, AND WE'D HAD SAD ARGUMENTS LIKE THIS ONE —

IT HAD STARTED WITH A PHOTO IN THE CATHOLIC WEEKLY OF A DUSTBIN-LINER FULL OF ABORTED BABIES — HERE'S SOMETHING SIMILAR —

YOU CAN'T HAVE HALF AN ABORTION...YOU HAVE TO BE ON ONE SIDE OR THE OTHER— YOU CAN'T GO THROUGH LIFE WITH YOUR EYES CLOSED!

HOW CAN YOU HAVE NO OPINION AT ALL ABOUT SOMETHING THIS SERIOUS?!

Hands Off!

DANNY GREY'S MOTHER USED TO BE THE DISTRICT NURSE IN HOCKLEY AND DANNY OFTEN ESCORTED HER THROUGH THE WOODS TO LAY OUT A DEAD PERSON IN SOME HOUSE OR OTHER.

DANNY SAYS HE'D SEEN MORE CORPSES BEFORE HE WAS SIXTEEN THAN MOST OF US SEE IN A LIFETIME.

Alec · Book 2 · page 36

HAVING NO INFLUENCE ONE WAY OR THE OTHER IN MATTERS OF LIFE;
THAT IS, NOT BEING FATHER, MIDWIFE, MURDERER, GOVERNMENT
FIRE-SAFETY INSPECTOR, I'M GOING ALONG VOICING EFFETE
PHILOSOPHIES ON THE SUBJECT.

LIFE IS JUST PASSING TIME TILL THE TRAIN COMES IN -

AH, BUT WHICH WAY IS THE TRAIN GOING? - AND CAN YOU LET IT GO AND WAIT FOR A LATER ONE?

IT'S ONLY A METAPHOR... ANYWAY, I WAS TRYING TO BE FUNNY, NOT PASS A BLOODY PARLIAMENTARY BILL -

AS A PHILOSOPHER YOU'RE HUMOROUS.

AS IT HAPPENED I DIDN'T VISIT MY PARENTS AGAIN FOR OVER A YEAR, AND NOT BECAUSE OF THOSE DISAGREEMENTS, MINISCULE THINGS IN FACT.

...BUT BECAUSE OF A NEW PREOCCUPATION IN MY LIFE, WHICH CAME ALONG AT THE END OF THE MAYDAY BANK HOLIDAY WEEKEND. BEAR WITH ME A COUPLE OF CHAPTERS; IT BEGINS LIKE THIS...

...AND THEN WE HAD A HELL OF A CONVERSATION ABOUT THE ABORTION QUESTION.

...AND I WOKE UP THE OTHER DAY WITH A PIECE OF ALMOST GOLDBERGIAN WISDOM IN MY HEAD

... WHATEVER WAY YOU BOUNCE IT, IT'S STILL A BABY

HELLO, DARLINGS... I NEED YOUR HELP, DANNY.

HI LOUISE

REMEMBER MY UNCLE ART? *uh...*

EASTER WEEKEND. HE WAS HERE, CAMPED OUTSIDE WITH HIS SPACE APPRENTICES *Air Training Cadets*

YES, WELL REMEMBER THE LITTLE PLAQUE HE AWARDED US FOR LETTING THEM USE THE FIELD AND YOU PROMISED HIM IT WOULD BE HUNG OVER THE BAR THE VERY NEXT DAY... *oh, I see.*

WELL HE'S COMING TONIGHT!

WE BETTER GET A HAMMER AND NAIL THEN. HAVE YOU GOT ANY? *no, darling*

AT JOHN GODFREY'S PLACE WE GET A HAMMER AND A CURTAIN-HOOK.

BUT THE PUB'S BUSTLING WHEN WE WALK BACK IN. ART'S ARRIVED AND HE'S LOOKING GLUM.

HI ART. KEEP 'IM BUSY, VIKKI!

IF I'M HONEST, I MUST RECORD THIS BIT.

I HOPE YOU'RE RECORDING ALL THIS, MacGARRY - 'IN THE DAYS OF THE KING CANUTE'

...IN EFFECT, CASTING A GLANCE AT THE FUTURE TO SAY "WHAT DO YOU THINK OF THIS, EH?" PICTURE OF A MAN PICTURING HIS PICTURE.

- YUP, I WAS JUST THINKING THE COMPOSITION REMINDS ME OF GERICAULT'S 'RAFT OF THE MEDUSA'.

SELF-CONSCIOUS, YES, BUT NOT AS IN PEOPLE'S "I COULD WRITE A BOOK ABOUT THIS PLACE" (BUT NEVER DO). DANNY NEVER KIDS HIMSELF THAT THE WRITING OF BOOKS REQUIRES ONLY THAT ONE HAS SEEN SOMETHING MEMORABLE.

HE LIVES HIS LIFE TO THE FULL.
NO PART IS SAVED LIKE
A SLICE OF BIRTHDAY CAKE
GOING STALE.

HE'S SELF-CONSCIOUS, BUT
NOT AS IN PEOPLE'S GOING AND
SEEING THE WORLD WITH THEIR
INEVITABLE RECORD OF IT;
PHOTO OF ME IN FRONT OF THE
STATUE OF LIBERTY...

...ME IN FRONT OF THE ARC DE
TRIOMPHE, ME BESIDE THE GUARD
AT BUCKINGHAM PALACE, NOT
SEEING THAT THE COMMON
DENOMINATOR IS THE ME...

...ME IN THE KITCHEN SINK.

I USED TO SIT IN THE GARDEN
PAINTING OILS OF RHUBARB
PATCHES AND FULL DUSTBINS
AND MY AUNT ASKED "WHY
DON'T YOU PAINT NICE SCENES?"

TO ME, THESE ARE THE
'NICE SCENES'. I MADE MENTAL
PICTURES, AND SOMETIMES PHOTOS
WHEN I TOOK TO HAVING A SMALL
CAMERA HANDY. THE GANG GOT
USED TO IT AND AFTER A WHILE
FORGOT TO POSE.

I HAD NO AMBITION BEYOND
LIFE'S DAILY ROUND AND THE
WEEKEND CELEBRATION OF IT.

THAT NIGHT LOUISE LETS DANNY
AND ME SLEEP IN THE ROOM
THAT USED TO BE THE
RESTAURANT.

BEDDING DOWN WARM I ALMOST
MAKE LOVE TO BELLA.

AND IN THE MORNING IN COMES
THE MORNING-COFFEE NYMPH.

IS THIS A BOTTLE IN FRONT O' ME OR A FRONTAL LOBOTOMY?

YAWN

A FAMOUS INTELLECTUAL WROTE THAT THE POWER OF ALCOHOL OVER MANKIND LIES IN ITS STIMULATION OF THE MYSTICAL FACULTIES OF HUMAN NATURE.

A FAMOUS GLASGOW DRUNK..(MY UNCLE GEORGE) SAID 'YOU WAKE UP THE NEXT MORNING WITH A SORE HEID AND A POCKET FULL OF STICKY PENNIES.

MY FATHER, ON THE OTHER HAND... ENCOURAGED ME TO DRINK IN AN 'EDUCATED' MANNER..I GUESS THAT'S WHY I'M AN EDUCATED DRUNK.

humm ... It's going to be another good day

HEY, WHERE DID ALL THESE BLANKETS COME FROM.?

LOUISE BROUGHT THEM DOWN.

OH OH...IT'S JUST COME BACK TO ME

huh.?

I WANDERED OUT TO THE LOO ABOUT FOUR O'CLOCK. I DIDN'T EVEN NOTICE THE LIGHT WAS ON.

OOPS

SORRY OH. OH, I EXPECT YOU'VE SEEN ONE BEFORE.

HOW CAN I FACE HER AGAIN? OH WELL, LET'S GET IT OVER WITH.

GOOD MORNING, LOUISE.

hmmm..DANNY! NOW I KNOW WHAT YOU'VE GOT. hee hee...

I'LL MAKE THE BREAKFAST. YOU HOOVER THE FLOOR AND GET A FIRE GOING.

WELL IT'S G.W. EARLY FOR YOU IS IT NOT?

GOOD MORNING, ALEC. TIMES CROSSWORD: FIVE, TWO, FOUR, FOUR: LISTEN INTENTLY TO SEXUAL DEVIATION...

GIVE IN.

PRICK UP ONE'S EARS

YOU MADE THAT UP!

HA HA HA

THAT'S IN THE SAME LEAGUE AS THE ONE SMIFFY CAME OUT WITH A WHILE AGO ON THIS VERY SPOT.

ALAS POOR YORLIK, I KNEW HIM BACKWARDS.

KILROY WAS HERE!

Well, well. DO I SMELL EGGS FRYING?

ALEC- BOOK 2 page 41

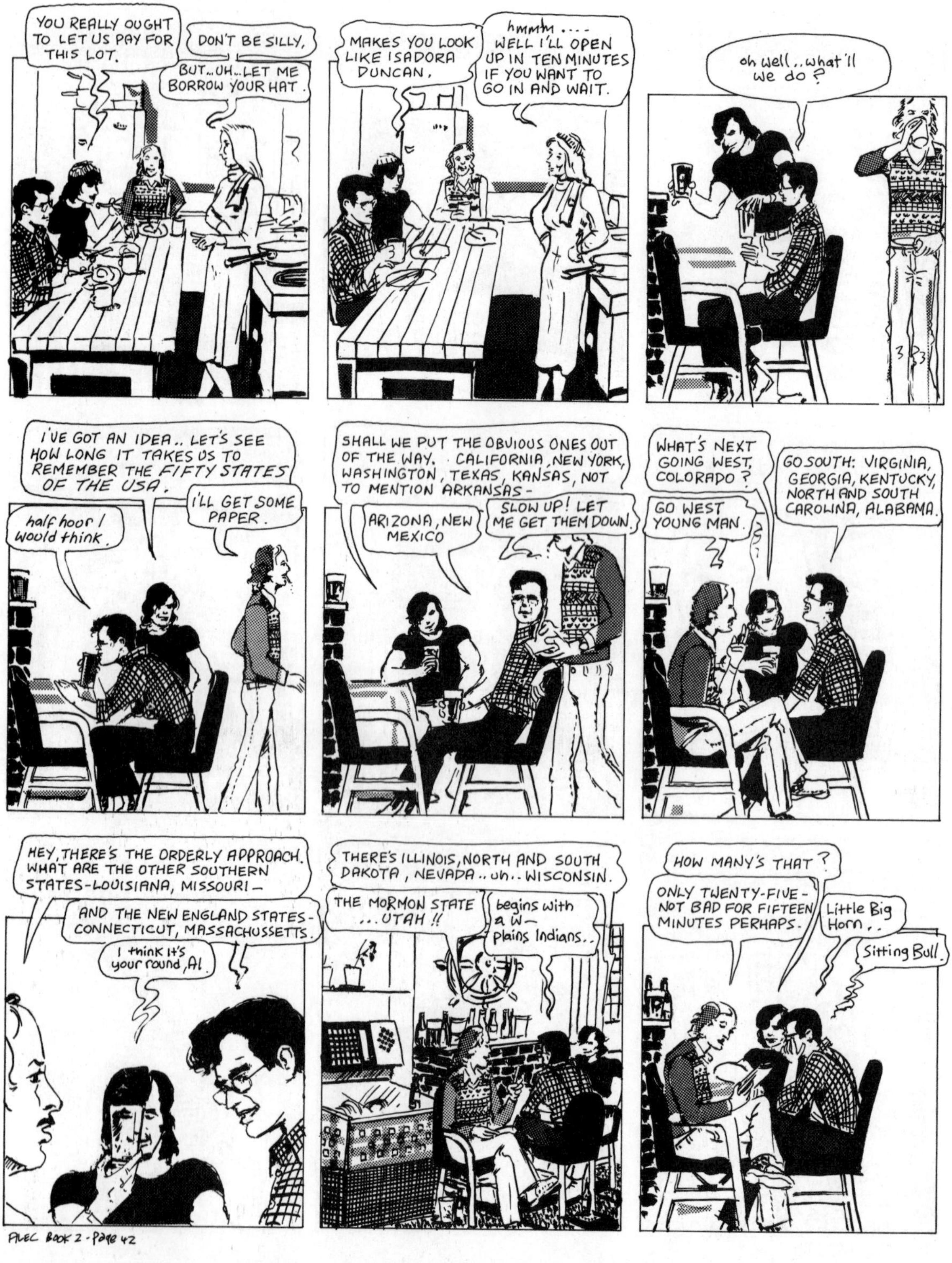
YOU REALLY OUGHT TO LET US PAY FOR THIS LOT.
DON'T BE SILLY,
BUT...UH...LET ME BORROW YOUR HAT.
MAKES YOU LOOK LIKE ISADORA DUNCAN.
hmmm.... WELL I'LL OPEN UP IN TEN MINUTES IF YOU WANT TO GO IN AND WAIT.
oh well,. what'll we do?
I'VE GOT AN IDEA.. LET'S SEE HOW LONG IT TAKES US TO REMEMBER THE FIFTY STATES OF THE USA.
half hour I would think.
I'LL GET SOME PAPER.
SHALL WE PUT THE OBVIOUS ONES OUT OF THE WAY. CALIFORNIA, NEW YORK, WASHINGTON, TEXAS, KANSAS, NOT TO MENTION ARKANSAS-
ARIZONA, NEW MEXICO
SLOW UP! LET ME GET THEM DOWN.
WHAT'S NEXT GOING WEST, COLORADO?
GO WEST YOUNG MAN.
GO SOUTH: VIRGINIA, GEORGIA, KENTUCKY, NORTH AND SOUTH CAROLINA, ALABAMA.
HEY, THERE'S THE ORDERLY APPROACH. WHAT ARE THE OTHER SOUTHERN STATES-LOUISIANA, MISSOURI-
AND THE NEW ENGLAND STATES-CONNECTICUT, MASSACHUSSETTS.
I think it's your round, Al.
THERE'S ILLINOIS, NORTH AND SOUTH DAKOTA, NEVADA.. uh.. WISCONSIN.
THE MORMON STATE ...UTAH!!
begins with a W- plains Indians..
HOW MANY'S THAT?
ONLY TWENTY-FIVE-NOT BAD FOR FIFTEEN MINUTES PERHAPS.
Little Big Horn,.
Sitting Bull.

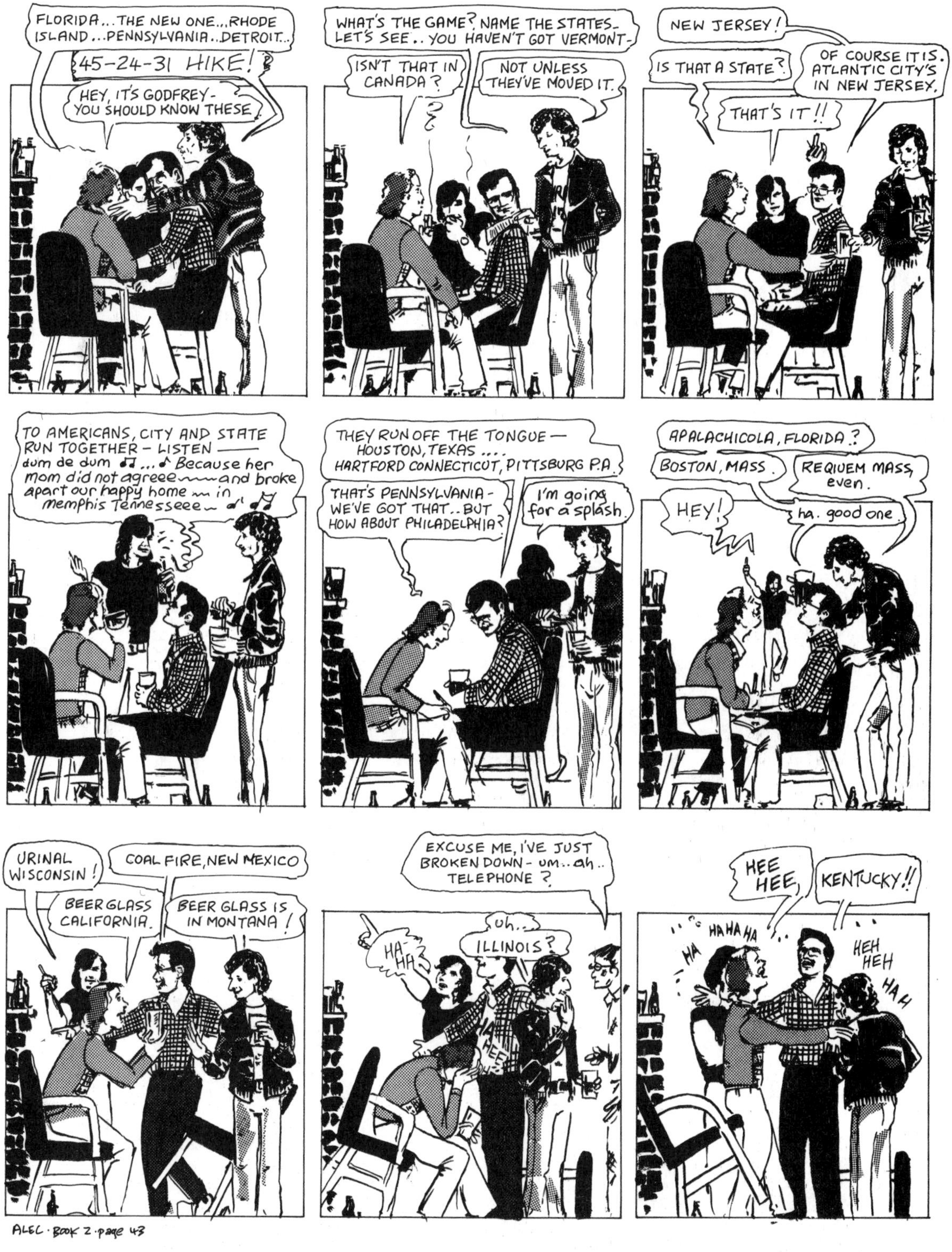
FLORIDA... THE NEW ONE... RHODE ISLAND... PENNSYLVANIA.. DETROIT...
45-24-31 HIKE!
HEY, IT'S GODFREY- YOU SHOULD KNOW THESE.
WHAT'S THE GAME? NAME THE STATES- LET'S SEE.. YOU HAVEN'T GOT VERMONT-
ISN'T THAT IN CANADA?
NOT UNLESS THEY'VE MOVED IT.
NEW JERSEY!
IS THAT A STATE?
OF COURSE IT IS. ATLANTIC CITY'S IN NEW JERSEY.
THAT'S IT!!
TO AMERICANS, CITY AND STATE RUN TOGETHER - LISTEN —— dum de dum ... Because her mom did not agreee and broke apart our happy home in memphis Tennesseee
THEY RUN OFF THE TONGUE — HOUSTON, TEXAS .... HARTFORD CONNECTICUT, PITTSBURG P.A.
THAT'S PENNSYLVANIA - WE'VE GOT THAT.. BUT HOW ABOUT PHILADELPHIA?
I'm going for a splash.
APALACHICOLA, FLORIDA?
BOSTON, MASS.
REQUIEM MASS, even.
HEY!
ha. good one.
URINAL WISCONSIN!
COAL FIRE, NEW MEXICO
BEER GLASS CALIFORNIA.
BEER GLASS IS IN MONTANA!
EXCUSE ME, I'VE JUST BROKEN DOWN - um.. ah.. TELEPHONE?
HA-HA
uh..
ILLINOIS?
HEE HEE,
KENTUCKY!!
HA HA HA HA
HA
HEH HEH
HAH

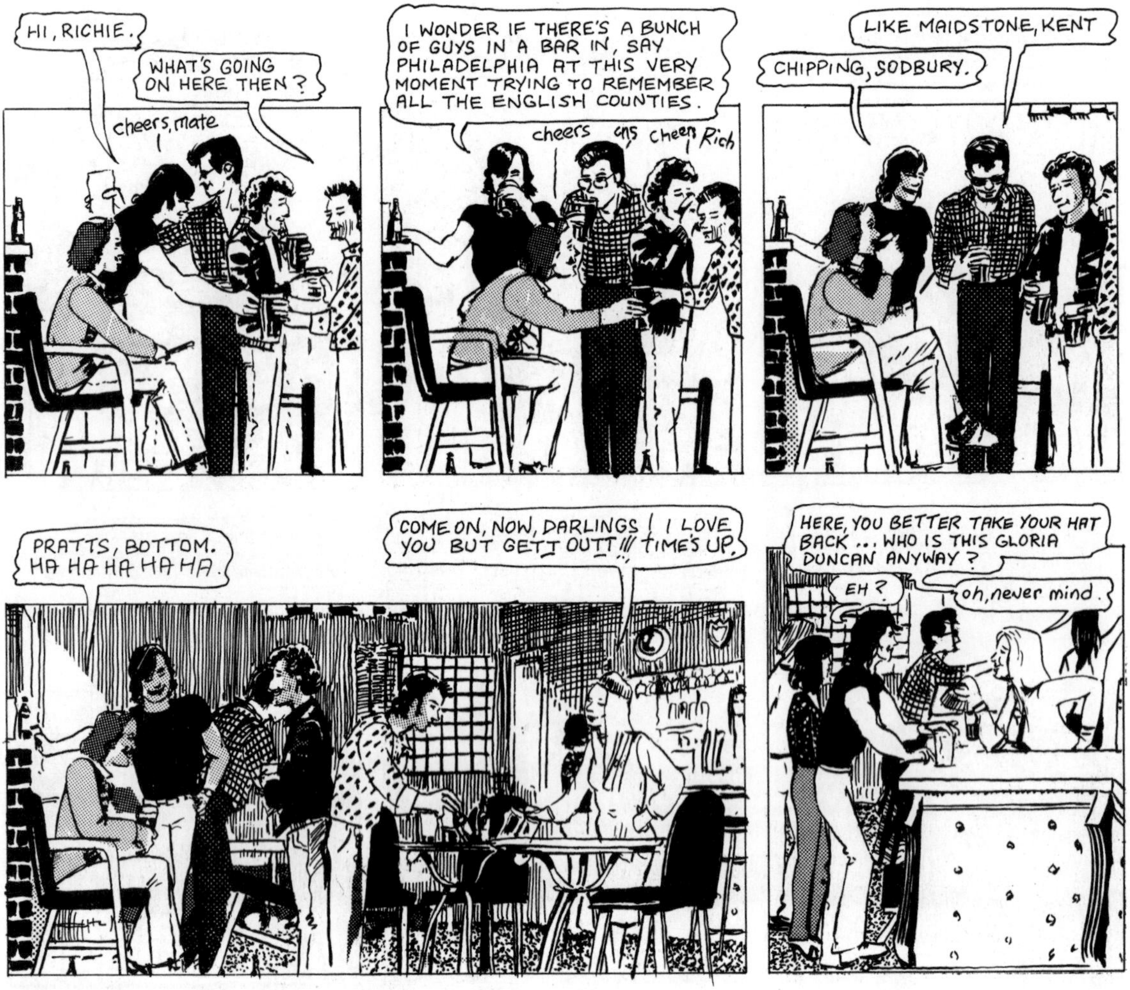
HI, RICHIE.
WHAT'S GOING ON HERE THEN?
cheers, mate
I WONDER IF THERE'S A BUNCH OF GUYS IN A BAR IN, SAY PHILADELPHIA AT THIS VERY MOMENT TRYING TO REMEMBER ALL THE ENGLISH COUNTIES.
cheers
chs
Cheers Rich
CHIPPING, SODBURY.
LIKE MAIDSTONE, KENT
PRATTS, BOTTOM. HA HA HA HA HA.
COME ON, NOW, DARLINGS! I LOVE YOU BUT GETT OUTT!!! TIME'S UP.
HERE, YOU BETTER TAKE YOUR HAT BACK ... WHO IS THIS GLORIA DUNCAN ANYWAY?
EH?
oh, never mind.

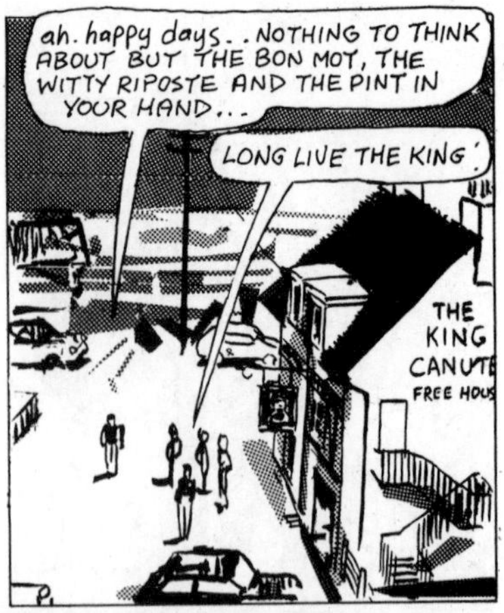
ah. happy days.. NOTHING TO THINK ABOUT BUT THE BON MOT, THE WITTY RIPOSTE AND THE PINT IN YOUR HAND...
LONG LIVE THE KING!
THE KING CANUTE FREE HOUS

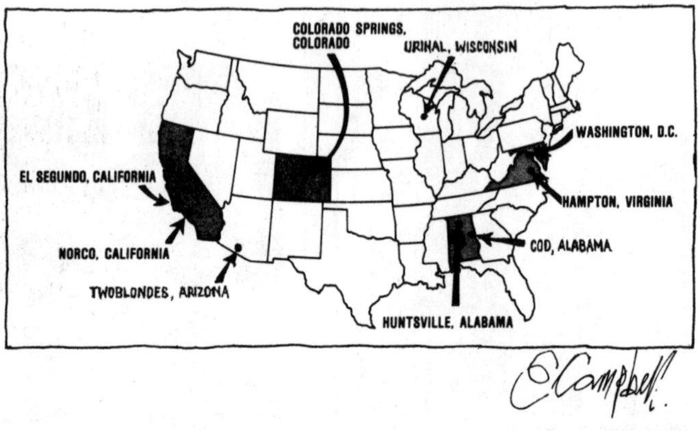
COLORADO SPRINGS, COLORADO
URINAL, WISCONSIN
WASHINGTON, D.C.
EL SEGUNDO, CALIFORNIA
HAMPTON, VIRGINIA
COD, ALABAMA
NORCO, CALIFORNIA
TWOBLONDES, ARIZONA
HUNTSVILLE, ALABAMA

E Campbell

A PERMANENT FEATURE OF THE KING CANUTE IS A BUNCH OF GUYS WHO PARK THEIR BIKES ON THE PORCH.

AND LEAVE THEIR 'SKID-LIDS' ON THE MANTLEPIECE.

AND SAY THINGS I DON'T UNDERSTAND LIKE—

THE 900 CRANK IS FASTER—

YOU HAVE TO DRILL HOLES IN THE PINS—

Dave Pooles been building bikes for as long as I remember

THERE'S NICK LAING, JUST BACK FROM AUSTRALIA, AND HIS LONG-TIME GIRL-FRIEND MONICA; THERE'S THE VIKING AND OTHER CHARACTERS—

PARTY IN HOCKLEY— YOU MUST ALL COME.

MY PALS ARE DIVIDED ON THE MATTER OF GOING TO THIS PARTY AND WANDER IN AND OUT OF DAVE TIMMINS' ROOM—

— WE COULDN'T GET A TAXI—

KEN JUST PHONED US TO COME ALONG TO THE PARTY? WHO'S GAME?

I'M NOT TOO HEAVY, ALEC?

LIKE WEARING A THICK VEST.

hmm- oh, he's got a good grip on the curves.

(le printemps)

picasso

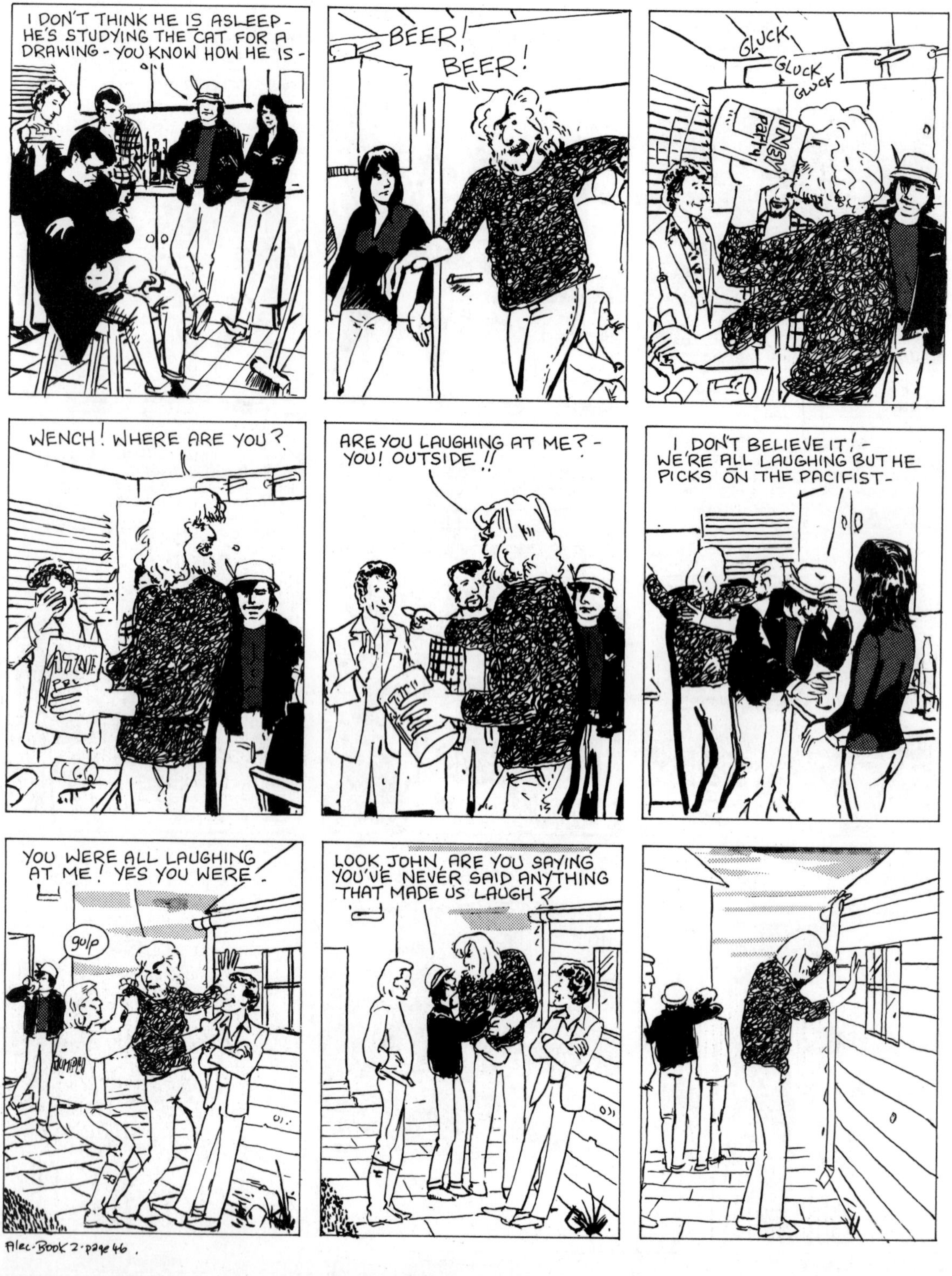
I DON'T THINK HE IS ASLEEP - HE'S STUDYING THE CAT FOR A DRAWING - YOU KNOW HOW HE IS -
BEER!
BEER!
GLUCK
GLUCK
GLUCK
WENCH! WHERE ARE YOU?
ARE YOU LAUGHING AT ME? - YOU! OUTSIDE!!
I DON'T BELIEVE IT! - WE'RE ALL LAUGHING BUT HE PICKS ON THE PACIFIST -
YOU WERE ALL LAUGHING AT ME! YES YOU WERE.
gulp
LOOK, JOHN, ARE YOU SAYING YOU'VE NEVER SAID ANYTHING THAT MADE US LAUGH?

Alec-Book 2-page 46.

I HAVE ENTERED INTO A TWILIGHT WORLD OF DRUNKENNESS NOW, A LAND OF FAERIE THAT STILL SPARKLES IN THE LIGHT OF DAY.

A HOLY FEW HOURS IN WHICH I WILL FALL IN LOVE, AMONG OTHER THINGS.

YOU HAVE BELITTLED ME!!

I'D GONE TO SLEEP BECAUSE I'D HAD MY FILL, AND MORE—I WAS FED UP, READY TO CHANGE MY LIFESTYLE IF I COULD JUST GET HOME FOR 12 HOURS KIP.

BUT AS I PRESSED AHEAD ONE SENSATION PILED ON ANOTHER WITHOUT ANY LOGICAL PRO-GRESSION AND I AM 'DRUNK' ON THESE—

THE VIKING, RATTLER OF WHOLE GARAGE WITH HIS NUT; SMIFFY, DICER WITH DOGSHIT; DANNY GREY, ROUNDER UP OF TWO HUNDRED AND FIFTY SHEEP—

AND KNOWER OF COUNTRY THINGS—

IT'S GOING TO BE A FINE DAY.

HOW CAN YOU TELL?

THERE HAS TO BE HEAT TO BRING ALL THIS MIST UP—

FIVE O'CLOCK BACK IN TIMMINS' ROOM—LOOKING AT TEETH, POTENTIAL NO-TEETH IN BOOZY NEGLIGENCE (I EXAGGERATE BUT IT'S MY PARTICULAR ANXIETY)

GO TO SLEEP FR FKSAKE

..SORT OF LITTLE-GETHSEMANE GRIEF WITH DANNY GREY LOATH-SOME DRUNK ASLEEP WITH HIS UGLY HAT ON—I WANT TO STEP ON HIS HEAD.

HOURS LATER, GEORGE AND VICKI

SO I SAID WHAT ABOUT THE REST?

AND I REPLIED WHAT ABOUT A REST?

GEORGE TRANSPORTS THE
RITUAL GLASS OF BEER UPSTAIRS

LOUISE COMES IN FROM THE
GARDEN WITH A BABY WRAPPED
IN SPRING TREES...

AND IN THIS FIRST SUNDAY DINNER
MOMENT I, RECORDER AND
REMEMBERER OF THESE THINGS,
TAKE A PHOTO—

THE FIRST AND UNEQUALLED, OF
DANNY GREY— GABRIEL TOUSLED
CLEANSHAVEN SHEPHERD FACE—

AND SPEAKING OF BABES, IN
WALKS MINE—(ACTUALLY NOT
QUITE LIKE THAT, AMERICAN
TOUGH GUY PRIVATE-EYE SORT OF
INTRODUCTION)

PENNY AND ANGELINE IN FACT
ARRIVED A LITTLE EARLIER,
SAW US FROM THE LOUNGE BAR
AND CAME THROUGH—

PENNY MOORE, HOCKLEYWOOD
RIDING FACED, MIDNIGHT WINK
EYELASHES, THE SUN ALL
CAUGHT UP IN HER HEAD—

AND THERE MUST HAVE BEEN
SQUIRRELS IN BROWN GLASS
BOTTLE BRANCHES UP
BEHIND THE BAR.

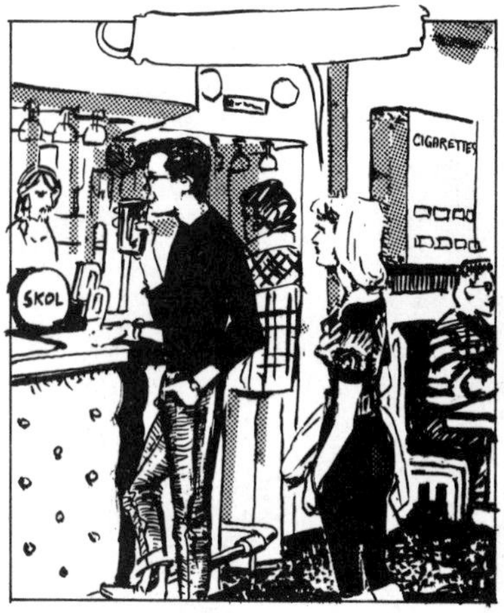
CIGARETTES
SKOL

BOOK THREE

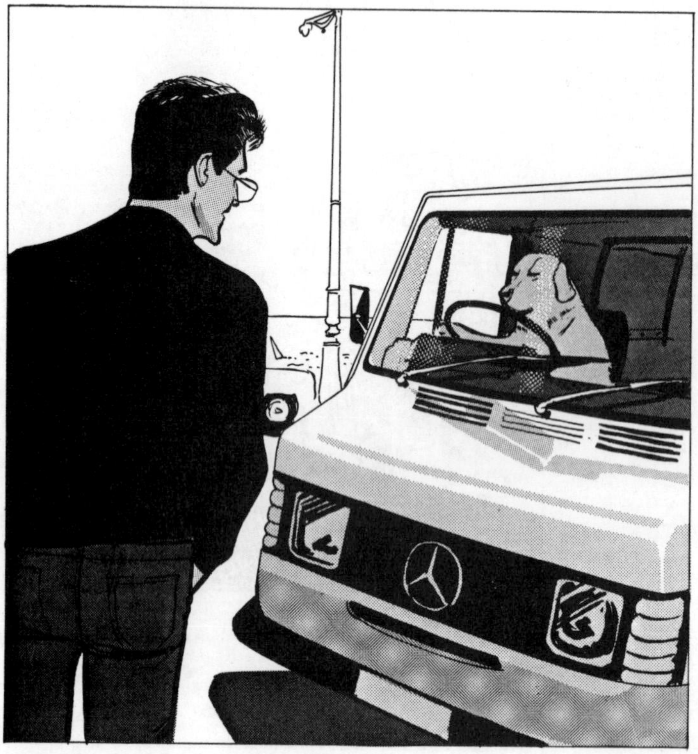

DOGGIE IN THE WINDOW.

A FUNNY NOTION OCCURRED TO ME WHILE I WAS DROWNING.

I SAW HUMANITY ALL PASTED TOGETHER WITH SEMEN.

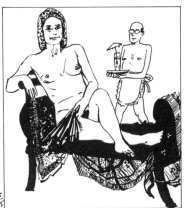

IT WAS RUNNING DOWN LEGS AT BUS STOPS AFTER EARLY MORNING QUICKIES.

IT WAS DRIPPING OFF THE ENDS OF NOSES.

THE WORD 'SPUNK' IS GOOD ENGLISH, I HAVE ALWAYS THOUGHT, AT LEAST ACCORDING TO THE DANNY GREY PRINCIPLE, WHERE *shithouse* IS BETTER ENGLISH THAN *lavatory*

la-va-tri
yech— bad

WARM AND STICKY. BUT OF COURSE ANGELINE AND ELLEN AREN'T THINKING ABOUT IT IN THOSE TERMS WHILE THEY'RE PADDING FIERCELY ROUND EACH OTHER...

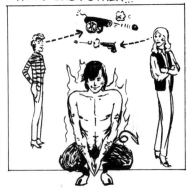

TRYING TO WIN HIS TIME.

?

MY MOTHER NEITHER, BUT IT'S ALL SEX. THE UNIFYING ELEMENT. IT SERVES ITS PURPOSE.

LIKE THIS PREAMBLE, WHERE I REMIND YOU WHO'S WHO IN THIS BIG CARTOON STORY I STARTED FIVE YEARS AGO. SO NEXTLY THERE'S GEORGE...

Alec· book 3· page 1

DANNY AND GEORGE WAKE UP IN A BEDSETTEE GEORGE WAS SUPPOSED TO BE DELIVERING SOMEWHERE —(ARE WOKE UP BY A PASSING COP ACTUALLY)— AND LOUISE'S BIG ST. BERNARD RAN OFF WITH ONE OF DANNY'S BOOTS IN THE NIGHT—

LOUISE, THERE ARE TWO MEN SLEEPING ON THE PORCH

AROUND THIS TIME LOUISE'S NIECE VICKI FIELDING WAS WORKING WEEKENDS AT THE CANUTE, HOOVERING THE CARPET AND WASHING GLASSES —

GEORGE GAVE HER A LIFT HOME THAT NIGHT AFTER THE BEDSETTEE.

PURSUING THE MATTER FURTHER VICKI GOT GEORGE'S PHONE NUMBER FROM ONE OF THE GUYS BUT DIDN'T HAVE THE COURAGE TO PHONE HIM HERSELF.

LOUISE DID AN IMPERSONATION—(SHE'S ONE OF THE OWNERS OF THE PUB, I FORGOT TO MENTION —)

SO IN NO TIME AT ALL GEORGE WAS STAYING WEEKEND NIGHTS WITH VICKI IN HER OCCASIONAL ROOM UPSTAIRS.

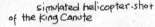

simulated helicopter-shot of the King Canute

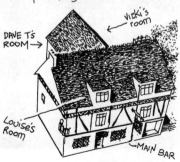

VICKI'S ROOM

DAVE T'S ROOM →

LOUISE'S ROOM

MAIN BAR

DANNY WOULD SLEEP IN THE ROOM DAVE TIMMINS RENTS AND ON WEEKEND MORNINGS THEY'D ALL BE IN THE BAR REAL EARLY, WITH GEORGE PLAYING

FOR HE'S A FELLY GOOD JOLLO

OF COURSE, I DON'T KNOW HOW OTHER PEOPLE'S SEX GOES, THOUGH A FEW PERSONAL OUTINGS MAY GIVE ONE A GENERAL IDEA OF THE TENOR OF THE MODERN FUCK.

MAYBE THEY EMPLOY A VAST ARRAY OF *MARITAL AIDS*.

OR DO THE DEED WITH A MODICUM OF RESTRAINT AND GOOD TASTE.

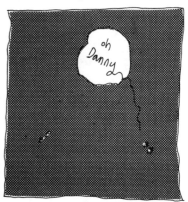

oh Danny

OR MAYBE LIKE GETTING THE ENGINE OUT OF THE CAR, TELLING JOKES ALL THE WHILE.

OR MAYBE SOMEBODY I KNOW'S JERKING AWAY FOR DEAR LIFE AT THIS VERY MINUTE, ADDING ANOTHER VAIN DOLLOP TO THE WORLD'S SPUNK MOUNTAIN.

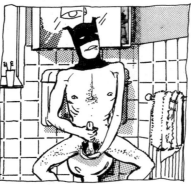

BUT GODDAMMIT, I'D SURE LIKE TO KNOW. NOBODY TELLS ANYBODY ANYTHING, OR AT LEAST NOT IN AN HONEST-TO-GOD SORT OF WAY (ME NEITHER, SO YOU CAN DISCOUNT EVERYTHING THAT FOLLOWS)

ALEC MacGARRY (me) AND PENNY MOORE INCH ACROSS THE BEDSIT FLOOR TILL WE'RE UNDER THE COOKER.

THOUGH I THINK I SHOVED THE QUILT DOWN.

I'M TRANSPORTED, PERHAPS TO THE BOTTOM OF THE RIVER CROUCH, SLOOPING ALONG, GRABBING UP MUD AS I GO

NEXT DAY, THE DAY OF THE HAT PARTY, SHE COMES INTO THE CANUTE AND HESITATES TO APPROACH.

THINKING PERHAPS NOW WE'VE DONE THE BUSINESS I'M MOVING ON (ME THINKING LIKEWISE SHE...

LATER IN THE WEEK WE GET ALL DRESSED UP FOR EACH OTHER WITH A COYNESS WE BOTH LATER FIND FUNNY.

(LOOKING BACK AT ALL THIS) I SEE PENNY IN CHANGES; IN AN OLD PHOTO AGE SEVENTEEN LIKE GREEK ATHENA.-

CENSORIOUS SEVERE MOTHER.

BUBBLING AUNT GIBBERISH.

blub

OUTDOORS TYPE RIDING.

MIDNIGHT SCHEMING.

(IN THE ALEXANDRA THAT NIGHT I COME FROM THE GENTS ROOM TO FIND A BIG IRISH DRUNK MOPPING HIS BROW WITH HER LITTLE MITT.

THIS —

I CAN'T GO IN THERE, ALEC. CYRIL'S IN THE BATH.

OH — THE SPIDER... IT'S BEEN IN THERE FOR DAYS. BILL SAID HE TRIED TO DROWN IT.. BUT IT DRANK ALL THE WATER —

WHO'S BILL ?
YOU KNOW, TWO DOORS AWAY

THE TWO THAT'S ALWAYS FIGHTING —
YUP — BILL AND COO ..

WHY COO ?
OHH... IT'S JUST AN OLD FASHIONED JOKE — IT'S WHAT PIGEONS DO.

WHY CYRIL ?

THIS TOO —

oh dear — I WAS SUPPOSED TO PICK MY MOTHER UP TO GO SHOPPING. —
TELL ME, WHY ARE YOU ALWAYS LATE ?

YOU DON'T KNOW THE HALF —.... THE DAY I SAT MY DRIVING TEST OR THE NIGHT BEFORE, I SHOULD SAY... I DISCOVERED MY PROVISIONAL LICENSE HAD EXPIRED .... SO THEY HAD TO PHONE HEADQUARTERS —

AND WHEN I'D JUST HAD PAULINE I REALIZED THAT ME AND JIM HADN'T EVEN THOUGHT OF A NAME — IT WAS THE NURSE THAT CAME UP WITH PAULINE

BUT ONLY THE THIRD NIGHT WE SPEND TOGETHER PENNY TALKS OF HER LOVER OF LAST EIGHTEEN MONTHS WHOM SHE HASN'T THE HEART TO TELL IT'S OVER.

IT ECHOES.

TWO WEEKS LATER THE GUY HAS A BIRTHDAY PARTY AT THE HOSPITAL (staff) AND PENNY'S BEEN ROUND THERE IN THE AFTERNOON MAKING THE SANDWICHES

MacGARRY KNOWS NOTHING ABOUT ALL THIS EXCEPT SHE'S GOING TO RUNWELL AND TO BOOT HE THOUGHT SHE SAID LONDON.

I WON'T SEE YOU THIS SATURDAY, ALEC -

huh ?

OH COME ON, DON'T SULK- hee hee —LOOK AT THE LIP ! WEE HUFFY MacGUFFY.

WHERE YOU OFF TO, THEN ?

London -

SO ALEC ARRANGES A NIGHT OUT WITH HIS BROTHER BRENDAN; THEY'RE ON THEIR WAY TO THE CANUTE WHEN BRENDAN'S CAR SHEDS A WHEEL.

ALEC'S ONLY THINKING OF THE PUB. SO HE PHONES A MESSAGE THROUGH. AND JOHN GODFREY COMES ALONG 5 MINUTES LATER.

I thought you'd be with Penny

not tonight

SHE WAS SUPPOSED TO MEET JOHN AND HER SISTER JEN AT THE CANUTE. SHE CAME LATE OF COURSE. OUR PATHS WOULD NOT HAVE CROSSED OTHERWISE.

SO IN I FALL.

OH, SO YOU SAID *RUNWELL*. -MM - O.K. YOU'LL WANT ME TO KEEP A LOW PROFILE THEN.

yes please

AT THE PARTY I FIND MYSELF WATCHING HER LIKE SHE'S MY PERSONAL PORTABLE THEATRE.

HEY, ALEC. I'M TALKING TO YOU.

SORRY JOHN - WHAT WAS IT?

AND THE OTHER FELLA. HE'LL PROBABLY CRY WHEN HE FINDS OUT WHAT'S ADRIFT. I WOULD TOO.

HE PROBABLY THOUGHT THERE WAS ONLY A SEMI-ESTRANGED HUSBAND TO DEAL WITH. I DID TOO.

AND MAYBE THAT HUSBAND FITS THE PICTURE BETTER THAN ME OR THE NURSE. JIM, A HEFTY GUY IN THE BUILDING TRADE, I'VE HEARD.

FOR PERHAPS ENTIRELY DUE TO MY INSECURITY, OR FROM SOME PREJUDICE ARISING FROM HER PEROXIDE BLONDENESS, I'D ENVISIONED HER WITH CONAN THE BARBARIAN.

OR SINBAD THE SAILOR OR ATTILLA THE HUN OR MICK McMANUS THE WRESTLER OR KEVIN THE DRUNK WITH THE WET BROW.

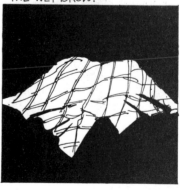

HOLLY SHERIDAN STARTED COMING INTO THE KING CANUTE WITH DAVE TIMMINS AROUND THE TIME OF THE HAT PARTY.

AND WAS PRESENT AT THE PECULIAR FALLING-OVER INCIDENT

IN WHICH TIMMINS AND DANNY GREY DRANK AROUND THE CLOCK.

DANNY WENT HOME AND DECANTED HIMSELF INTO THE BATH.

TIMMINS MADE A DASH FOR THE FINISH-LINE.

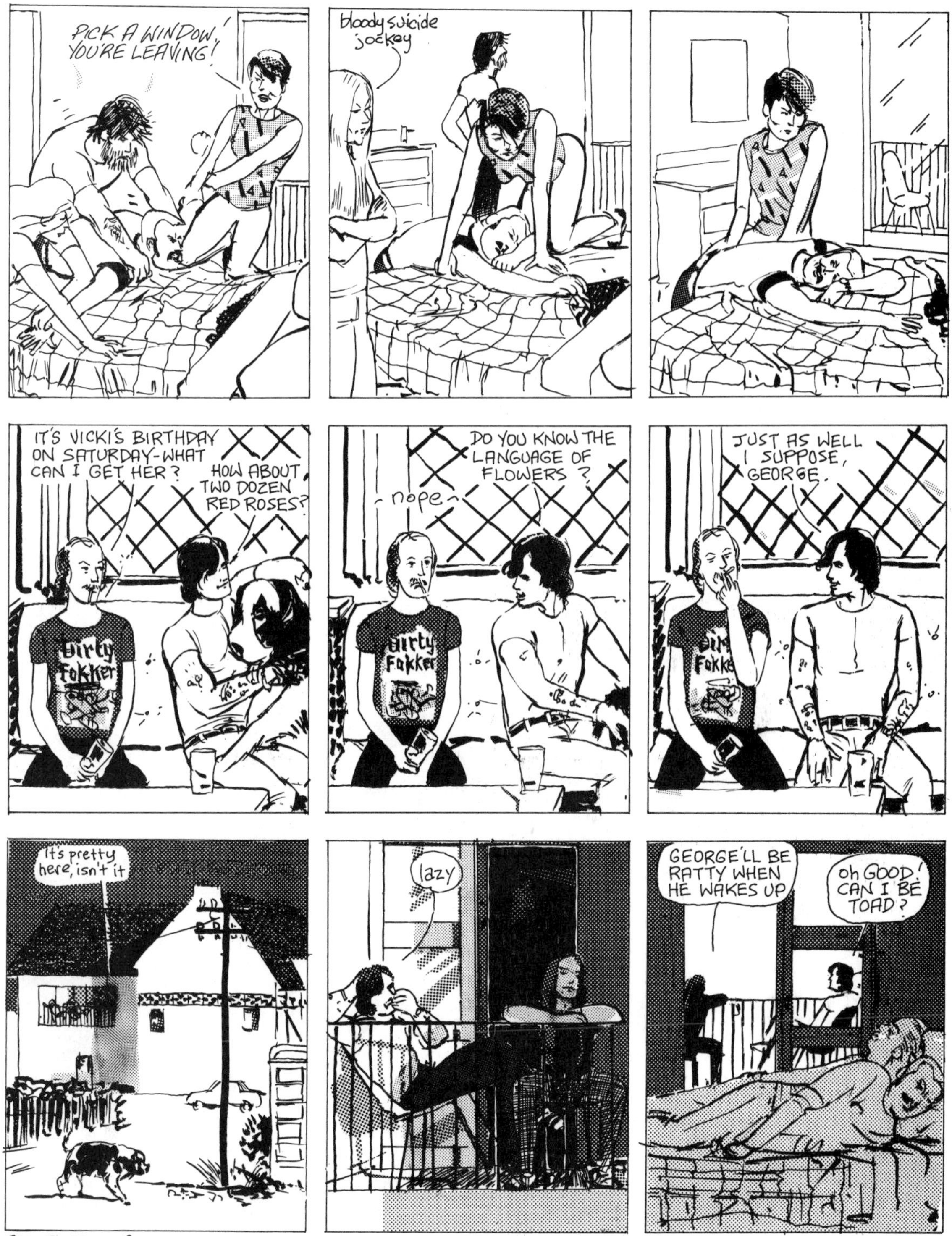
PICK A WINDOW, YOU'RE LEAVING!
bloody suicide jockey
IT'S VICKI'S BIRTHDAY ON SATURDAY - WHAT CAN I GET HER?
HOW ABOUT TWO DOZEN RED ROSES?
Dirty Fokker
DO YOU KNOW THE LANGUAGE OF FLOWERS?
- nope -
JUST AS WELL I SUPPOSE, GEORGE.
It's pretty here, isn't it
lazy
GEORGE'LL BE RATTY WHEN HE WAKES UP
oh GOOD! CAN I BE TOAD?

LOUISE HAS NICKNAMES FOR ALL HER TENANTS. AFTER THE FALLING OVER BUSINESS TIMMINS BECOMES 'THE SUICIDE JOCKEY'.

AND THE GUY NEXT DOOR- HE'S CALLED 'TABLES' BECAUSE WHEN HE FIRST COMES TO LOOK AT HIS ROOM.—

It's very nice but I think there should be a coffee table.. perhaps a bedside table — an occasional table...

GEORGE BECOMES A PAYING TENANT AT THIS TIME TOO AND MOVES ALL HIS THINGS IN UPSTAIRS. DANNY REMAINS AN UNOFFICIAL TENANT.

THEN THERE'S ELLEN, WHEN SHE DOES SOME PART-TIME WORK BEHIND THE BAR, MANY ARE HEARD TO OPINE THAT DANNY GREY HAS MET 'THE ONE'

HOWEVER, DANNY HAS BEEN SEEING A GREAT DEAL OF ANGIE OF LATE AND SHE IS GOING TO TAKE IT HARD.

AT THIS POINT BIG MICK TURNS UP.

ALEC- HAVE YOU MET MICK? - I HAVEN'T SEEN THIS GUY FOR 12 YEARS. HIM AND A PAL KNOCKED OVER A SUPERMARKET AND I WAS THE GETAWAY DRIVER.

YOU WON'T BELIEVE IT BUT THE HALFWITS COULDN'T RESIST WALKING PAST THE SCENE OF THE CRIME HALF AN HOUR LATER, WITH THEIR SHOES FULL OF POUND NOTES.

THERE I AM ASLEEP IN BED AND ME DAD COMES IN AND SHAKES ME —ALRIGHT, SON, WHAT HAVE YOU DONE? ~ NOTHING, DAD ~ THEN WHY ARE THERE COPS AT MY DOOR? —

PENNY AND I COMMIT THE POSSIBLY FORGIVEABLE ACT OF GIVING BIG MICK A LIFT THAT NIGHT AND TRYING TO PAIR HIM WITH ANGELINE.—NOBODY IS MINDING THEIR OWN BUSINESS.—

DANNY SPENDS THE NIGHT WITH ELLEN IN HER ROOM AT THE CANUTE.

AND EARLY NEXT MORNING IS PARTICIPATING IN HIS REGULAR SUNDAY SPORT.

THAT EVENING ~TIMMINS' ROOM.

DANNY! ELLEN'S DOWNSTAIRS— SHE SAYS IF YOU DON'T COME DOWN SOON SHE'S GOING OUT.

hmm

YOU CAN DO WITHOUT ME DANNY GREY. FIND YOURSELF A GIRL WHO LIKES CLIMBING TELEGRAPH POLES!!!

YOU OUGHT TO BE MORE RESPONSIBLE! YOU KNOW THAT MAN TIMMINS WOULD LEAP OFF A MOUNTAIN TO IMPRESS YOU.

THE LOGIC HERE SEEMS TO BE THAT DANNY IS A LEPRECHAUN WITH A CHARMED IMMORTALITY— BUT TIMMINS IS ONLY A MORTAL INSURANCE SALESMAN.

The bar in the sky

LOOK HERE!—DON'T GET STROPPY WITH ME AFTER ONE NIGHT!!!

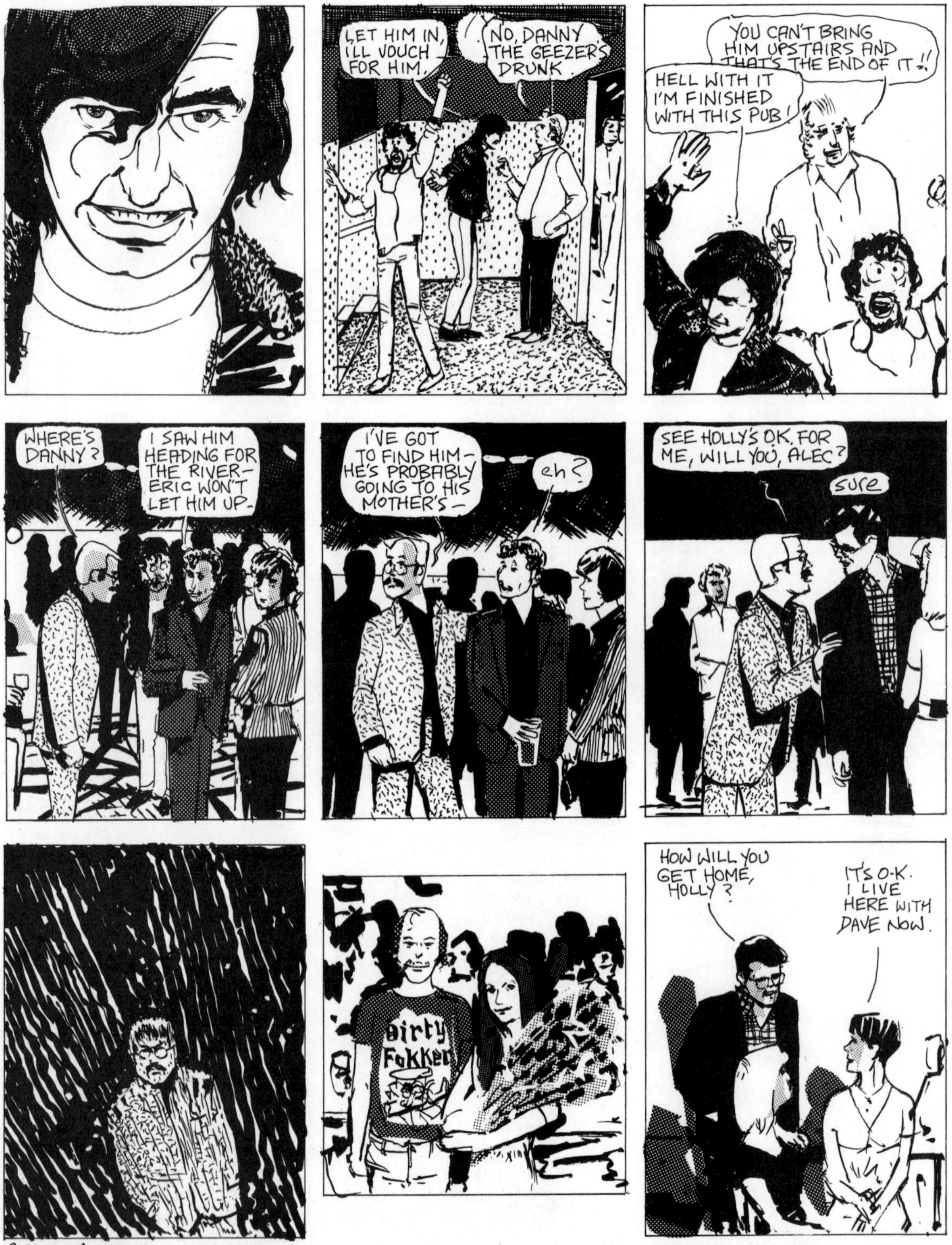
LET HIM IN, I'LL VOUCH FOR HIM.
NO, DANNY THE GEEZER'S DRUNK.
YOU CAN'T BRING HIM UPSTAIRS AND THAT'S THE END OF IT!!
HELL WITH IT I'M FINISHED WITH THIS PUB!
WHERE'S DANNY?
I SAW HIM HEADING FOR THE RIVER- ERIC WON'T LET HIM UP-
I'VE GOT TO FIND HIM- HE'S PROBABLY GOING TO HIS MOTHER'S-
eh?
SEE HOLLY'S O.K. FOR ME, WILL YOU, ALEC?
sure
Dirty Fokker
HOW WILL YOU GET HOME, HOLLY?
IT'S O.K. I LIVE HERE WITH DAVE NOW.

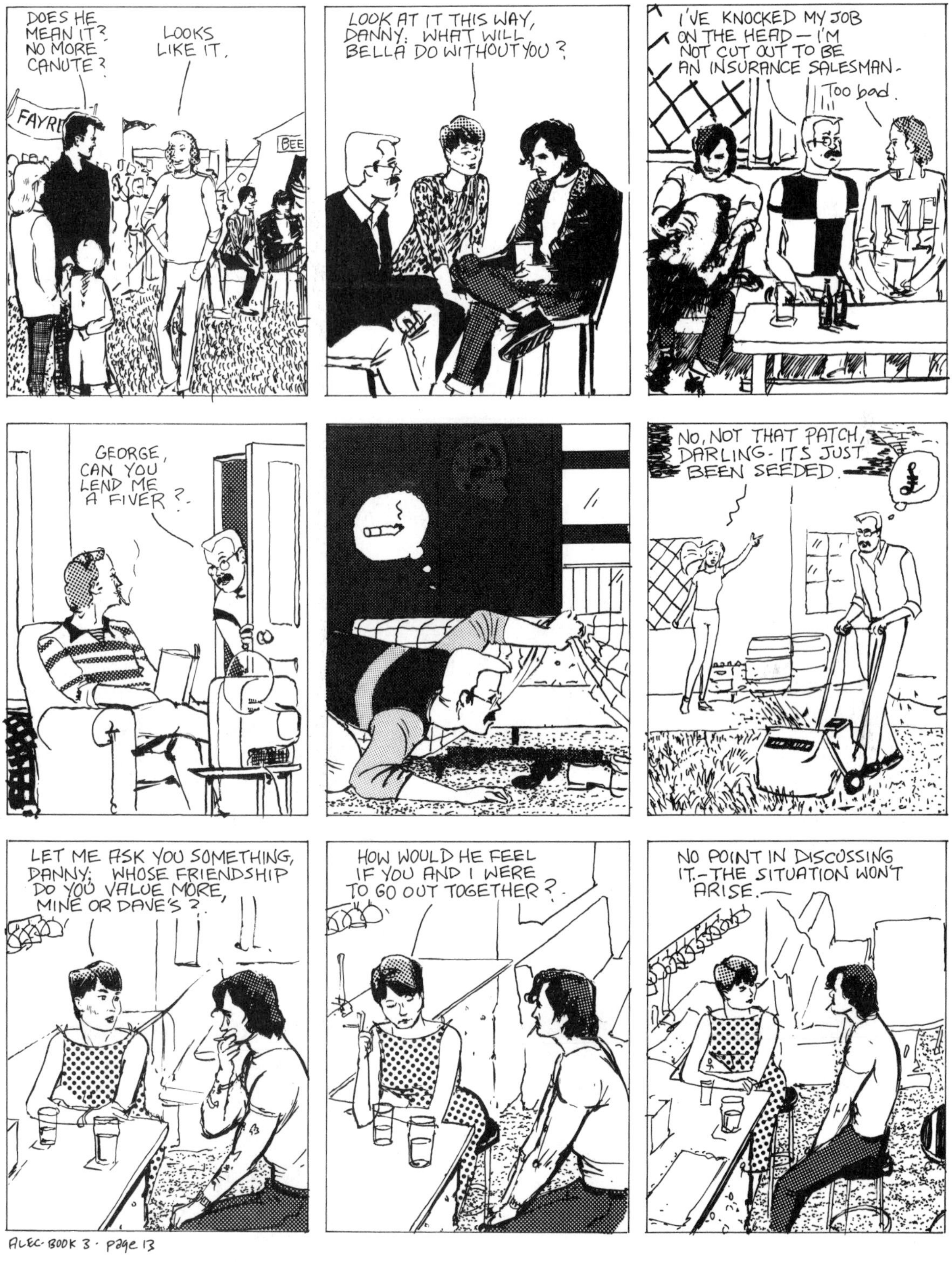
DOES HE MEAN IT? NO MORE CANUTE?
LOOKS LIKE IT.
FAYR
BEE
LOOK AT IT THIS WAY, DANNY: WHAT WILL BELLA DO WITHOUT YOU?
I'VE KNOCKED MY JOB ON THE HEAD — I'M NOT CUT OUT TO BE AN INSURANCE SALESMAN.
Too bad.
GEORGE, CAN YOU LEND ME A FIVER?
NO, NOT THAT PATCH, DARLING. IT'S JUST BEEN SEEDED.
£
LET ME ASK YOU SOMETHING, DANNY: WHOSE FRIENDSHIP DO YOU VALUE MORE, MINE OR DAVE'S?
HOW WOULD HE FEEL IF YOU AND I WERE TO GO OUT TOGETHER?
NO POINT IN DISCUSSING IT. — THE SITUATION WON'T ARISE.

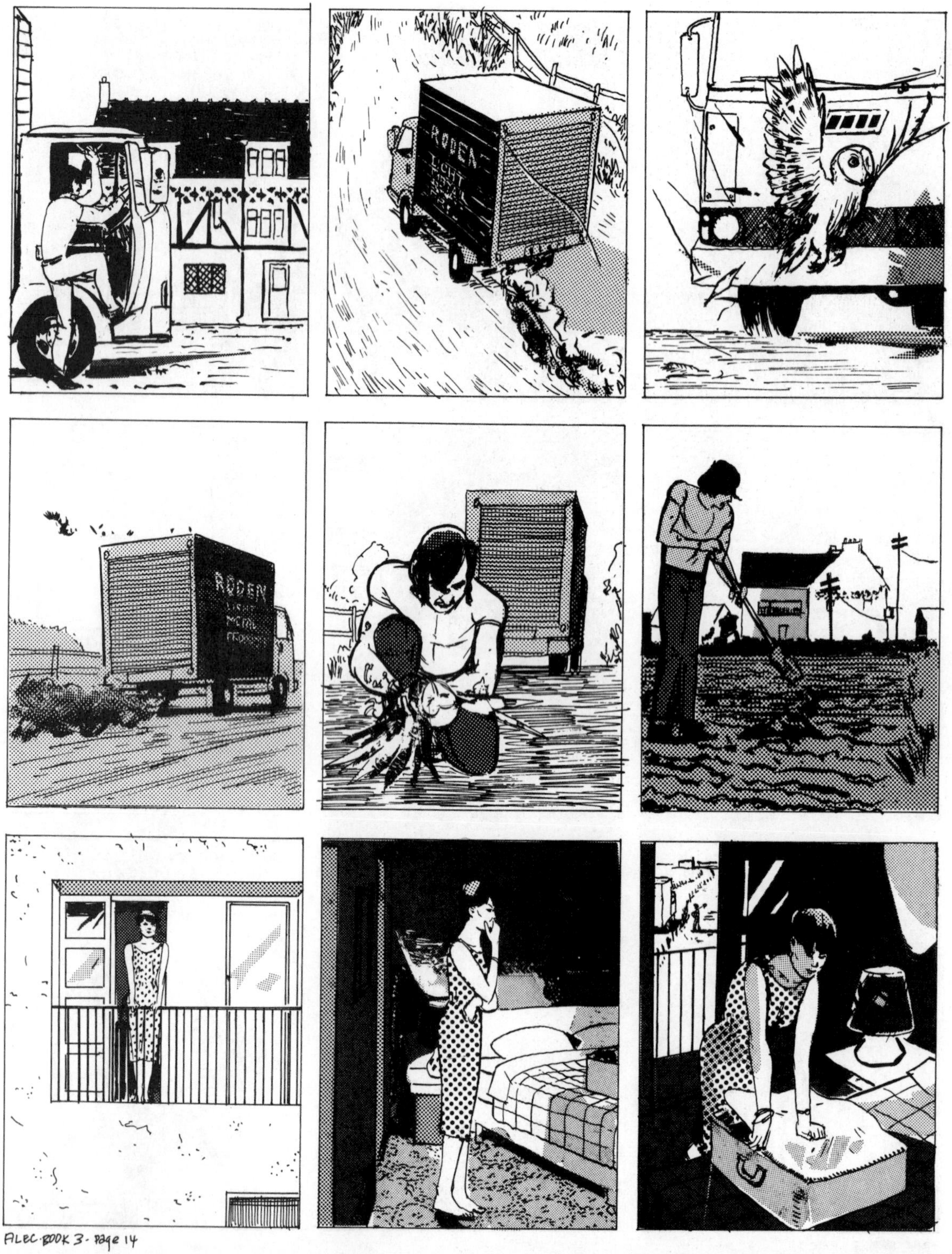
RODEN

NOW ALEC MacGARRY DOESN'T AS A RULE HAVE GUESTS SLEEP ON THE FLOOR. . BUT HIS BROTHER BRENDAN WAS WELL-GONE AND PAST CARING.

AND THE PREVIOUS NIGHT TOO— THAT WAS THE NIGHT THE WHEEL CAME OFF HIS CAR — BUT PENNY WAS THERE—

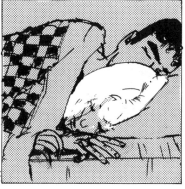

NEXT DAY, OVERDRESSED FOR SUNDAY MORNING, SHE HAD DROPPED THE BOYS OFF AT THE COACH FOR THE TRIP TO MARGATE ETC, ETC.

SO BLEAK MONDAY MORNING WHAT TO DO ABOUT THE CAR? PASSERBY OFFERS FIFTEEN QUID AND THAT'S THE END OF THE MATTER.

TUESDAY MORNING PENNY'S CAR IS NOW VERY TEMPERAMENTAL.

PENNY CONSEQUENTLY LATE HOME.

d o m e s t i c   I n t e r l u d e

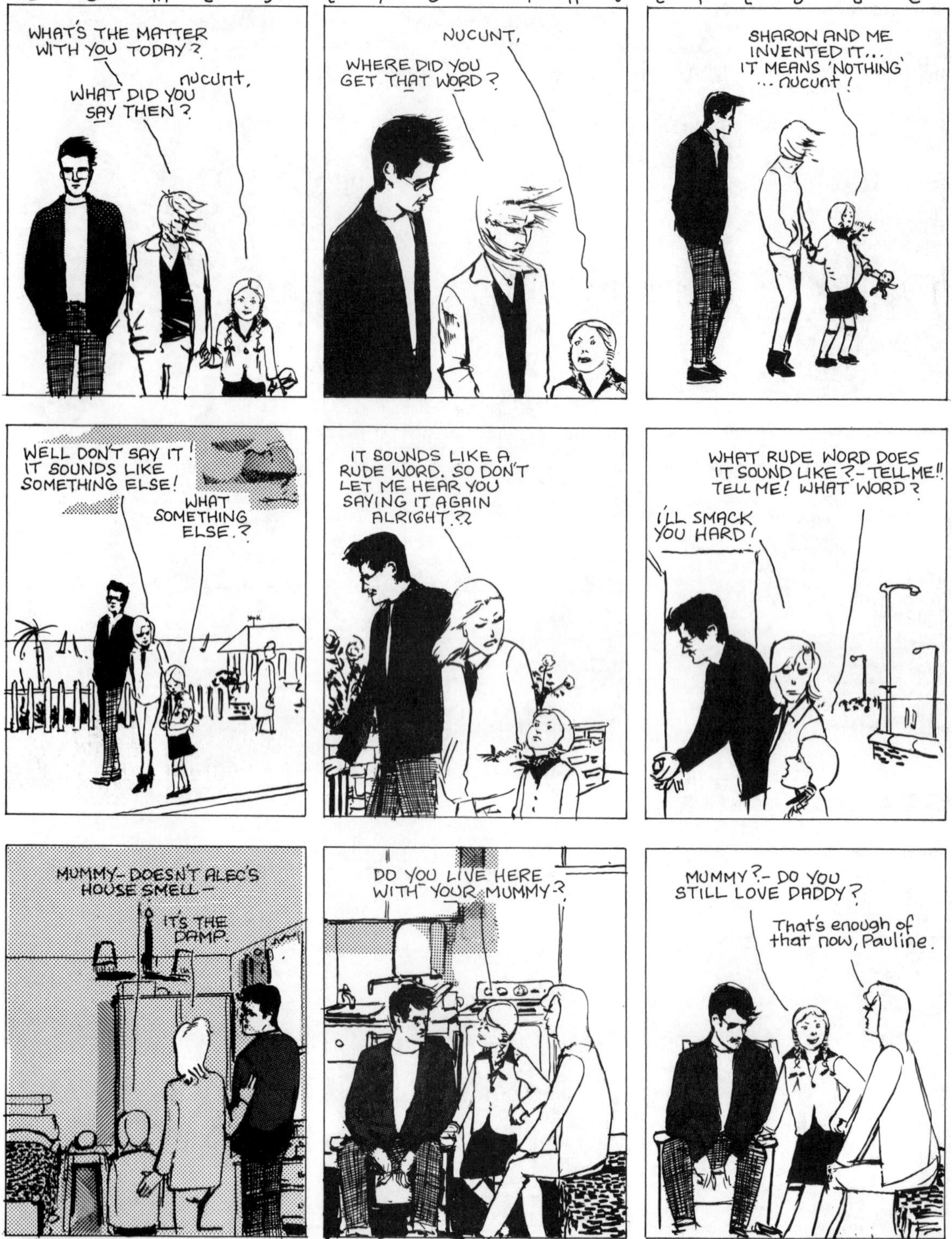

WHAT'S THE MATTER WITH YOU TODAY?
nucunt.
WHAT DID YOU SAY THEN?
NUCUNT.
WHERE DID YOU GET THAT WORD?
SHARON AND ME INVENTED IT... IT MEANS 'NOTHING' ... nucunt!
WELL DON'T SAY IT! IT SOUNDS LIKE SOMETHING ELSE!
WHAT SOMETHING ELSE?
IT SOUNDS LIKE A RUDE WORD. SO DON'T LET ME HEAR YOU SAYING IT AGAIN ALRIGHT??
WHAT RUDE WORD DOES IT SOUND LIKE?- TELL ME!! TELL ME! WHAT WORD?
I'LL SMACK YOU HARD!
MUMMY- DOESN'T ALEC'S HOUSE SMELL –
IT'S THE DAMP.
DO YOU LIVE HERE WITH YOUR MUMMY?
MUMMY?- DO YOU STILL LOVE DADDY?
That's enough of that now, Pauline.

ANOTHER NOTION OCCURRED TO ME~

WHERE DOES ONE'S SEXUALITY COME FROM— ?

IT'S NOT THERE AT THE BEGINNING LIKE HUNGER OR CURIOSITY

PLANTED LIKE LITTLE ACORNS SO TO SPEAK

BUT VISITS US QUITE BY SURPRISE

OOGA booga

TRANSFORMING US OVERNIGHT INTO SOMEONE ELSE

SOME FORMIDABLE CREATURE

AND DISAPPEARS JUST AS IT CAME

DISCONCERTINGLY

ALEC · BOOK 3 · page 17

DANNY AND I FELL IN WITH AUNT LUCY AND DICK LAST NIGHT AT THE PUB. WE END UP ROUND THEIR HOUSE.

THEIR DAUGHTER ANGELINE'S ALREADY GONE TO BED AND THERE'S A SWEET LITTLE FEMININE VOICE ON THE RADIO.

I DOZE OFF AND THINGS ARE SUPPOSED TO BE SAID THEN THAT LATER WILL CAUSE TROUBLE (THIS IS A LINE FROM THE FUTURE, IF YOU LIKE.)

SO WE'RE SLEEPING UPSTAIRS AND DANNY BUSTING HIS SEAMS AT THE MALEVOLENT GLARE ON ONE OF ANGIE'S OLD TEDDY-BEAR FACES.

YOU'RE ANNOYED I PHONED FROM AUNT LUCY'S THIS MORNING, AREN'T YOU.

YES — LOOK, FORGET IT — I DON'T WANT TO TALK ABOUT IT.

DANNY WAS THERE.

I DON'T CARE... — MY OWN COUSIN.

- - ?

I CAN'T FIGURE HER OUT. BUT THEN I'VE GOT A LOW PERSPECTIVE ON THESE THINGS...

I'M THE GLASWEGIAN ON THE FLOOR.

ALEC · BOOK 3 · page 18.

GEORGE WAITE WORKS AT THE AIRPORT AND THE CLUB OUTING THIS YEAR IS TO BE A DAY-FLIGHT TO LETOUQUET, FRANCE.

GEORGE MENTIONED IT IN THE PUB AND THAT THERE WERE SPARE SEATS SO OF COURSE I BAGGED A COUPLE FOR ME AND ANGELINE AS DID DAVE POOLE FOR LOUISE AND BORING DAVE FOR HOLLY.

LETOUQUET!

I'D LOVE TO GO TOO. ARE YOU SURE WE CAN'T WANGLE ANOTHER COUPLE OF PLACES?

THEY'VE ALL BEEN SNAPPED UP, ALEC. BUT I'LL DO MY BEST.

WHAT HAPPENS NEXT IS THAT DAVE TIMMINS AND HOLLY SPLIT UP.

HELLO VICKI. MAKE YOURSELF COMFORTABLE.

DAVE...HOLLY LEAVING DOESN'T CHANGE YOU IN OUR EYES, YOU KNOW.

YOU'LL ALWAYS BE THE SAME TO US: boring.

ALEC MacGARRY'S FLAT.

YEAH, THAT NIGHT HOLLY TOLD ME SHE WAS LEAVING, AND ASKED ME TO LOOK OUT FOR YOU.

Ha! What does she think I care about her or something?

DAVE TIMMINS ROOM AT THE KING CANUTE.

IT'S NOT GOING TO LOOK TOO GOOD TO LOUISE, DAVE. YOU GOING TO LETOUQUET AS THOUGH YOU CAN AFFORD THAT BUT NOT THE LAST THREE WEEKS' RENT.

YES, BUT I HATE TO LET GEORGE DOWN.

I THINK I MIGHT BE ABLE TO INTEREST ALEC AND PENNY IN GOING

YOU COULD?! THANKS!!

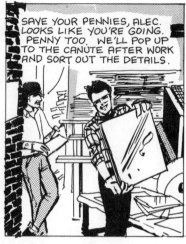

SAVE YOUR PENNIES, ALEC. LOOKS LIKE YOU'RE GOING. PENNY TOO. WE'LL POP UP TO THE CANUTE AFTER WORK AND SORT OUT THE DETAILS.

HEY, DANNY! I'M SORRY IF THIS SCREWS THINGS UP, BUT HOLLY SAYS WE'RE GOING AND SHE'S PAYING.

it's alright. I wasn't banking on it.

NO, NO. HOLD ON NOW, FOLKS.. THERE MUST BE A SOLUTION TO THIS ...um... yup... WHAT WE NEED IS A LARGE BOX... no, only kidding.. TWO OF US WILL HAVE TO TAKE THE FERRY AND THUMB FROM CALAIS.

..MYSELF AND ONE OF YOU.

I'M HAPPY TO THUMB.

NO! I'LL DO IT!!

YOU CAN BORROW MY ESCORT VAN.

TOO EXPENSIVE ON THE FERRY, LOUISE.

oh for heavens sake!!

I JUST PHONED HOLLY. WE'RE NOT GOING AND THAT'S THE END OF IT.

COME, COME, NOW.

WHAT DO YOU THINK, GEORGE?

I DON'T GIVE A SHIT WHO WALKS OR SWIMS. I JUST WANT YOU THREE TO ALL NOD IN AGREEMENT WHO'S GOING ON THE BLOODY PLANE!

HOLLY YOU'RE GOING!!

THE NEXT PROBLEM—

I THINK YOU CAN GO TO HELL, MISTER MacGARRY—

OH COME ON NOW—WHAT CAN I GET UP TO ON A HITCHIKING ADVENTURE?

THAT'S NOT IT!!

WHAT IS IT THEN?!

I've never flown before. I'm not going on my own O.K.?

THIS DEADLOCK RESOLVES ITSELF IN A PERFECTLY NATURAL MANNER AT THE CANUTE. DANNY DRIVES HOLLY UP THERE.

SHE'S UPSTAIRS DISCUSSING THE SITUATION WITH DAVE.

I'M GOING TO FERRY OVER THERE WITH MY FRIEND SHARON AND HITCH-HIKE LIKE DANNY AND ALEC—

WHILST IN THE LOUNGE BAR ANGELINE'S MOTHER, 'AUNT LUCY,' EXPRESSES A MORTAL FEAR OF FLYING.

I DON'T SEE WHY ALL OF YOU CAN'T HITCH-HIKE.

FURTHERMORE, SHE HAS ARRANGED TO HAVE A BIG PARTY ON THE SAME NIGHT AS THE TRIP AND WE'RE ALL INTENDING TO RUSH BACK TO IT.

only £8·60 for foot travellers on Thorsen.

IN THE MIDDLE OF ALL THIS, IN WALKS DAVE TIMMINS.

DANNY, COULD YOU RUN HOLLY HOME AGAIN?

Alec. Book 3 page 21

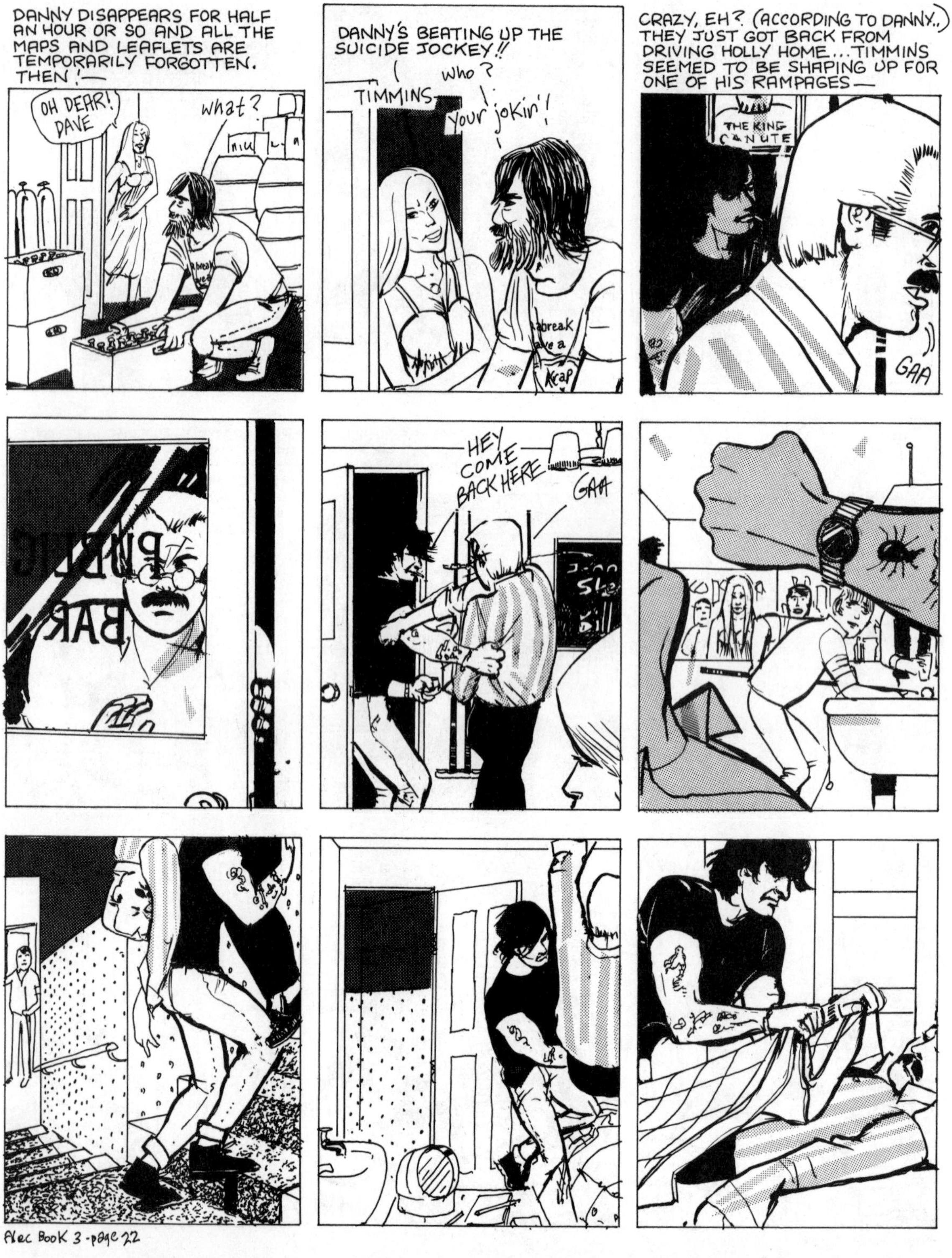
DANNY DISAPPEARS FOR HALF AN HOUR OR SO AND ALL THE MAPS AND LEAFLETS ARE TEMPORARILY FORGOTTEN. THEN!—
OH DEAR! DAVE
what?
DANNY'S BEATING UP THE SUICIDE JOCKEY!!
TIMMINS
who?
your jokin'!
CRAZY, EH? (ACCORDING TO DANNY..) THEY JUST GOT BACK FROM DRIVING HOLLY HOME... TIMMINS SEEMED TO BE SHAPING UP FOR ONE OF HIS RAMPAGES—
THE KING CANUTE
GAA
HEY COME BACK HERE
GAA

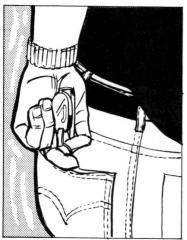

HEY

WHAT THE HELL'S GOING ON !!? YOU CAN'T GO BEATING PEOPLE UP HERE !!

LOOK I SAVED YOU AN UGLY SCENE IN YOUR BAR AND NOW I'M MISSING DRINKING TIME !!

ANYWAY. THERE HE IS, MATE. DOES HE LOOK BEAT UP ?

O.K O.K ~ FORGET IT, DANNY. I'LL BUY YOU A PINT COME ON.

SO THAT SORTS THAT OUT. DAVE AND HOLLY HAVE DECIDED NOT TO GO AND YOU AND I GET ON THE PLANE. I TOLD ANGELINE LAST NIGHT.

I'M GLAD YOU'RE COMING.

WHAT DIFFERENCE DOES IT MAKE ? IF THE PLANE GOES DOWN, I WON'T BE ABLE TO SAVE YOU.

WELL, WHAT MORE DO YOU WANT ME TO SAY—?

ANYWAY, I'VE NEVER FLOWN EITHER.

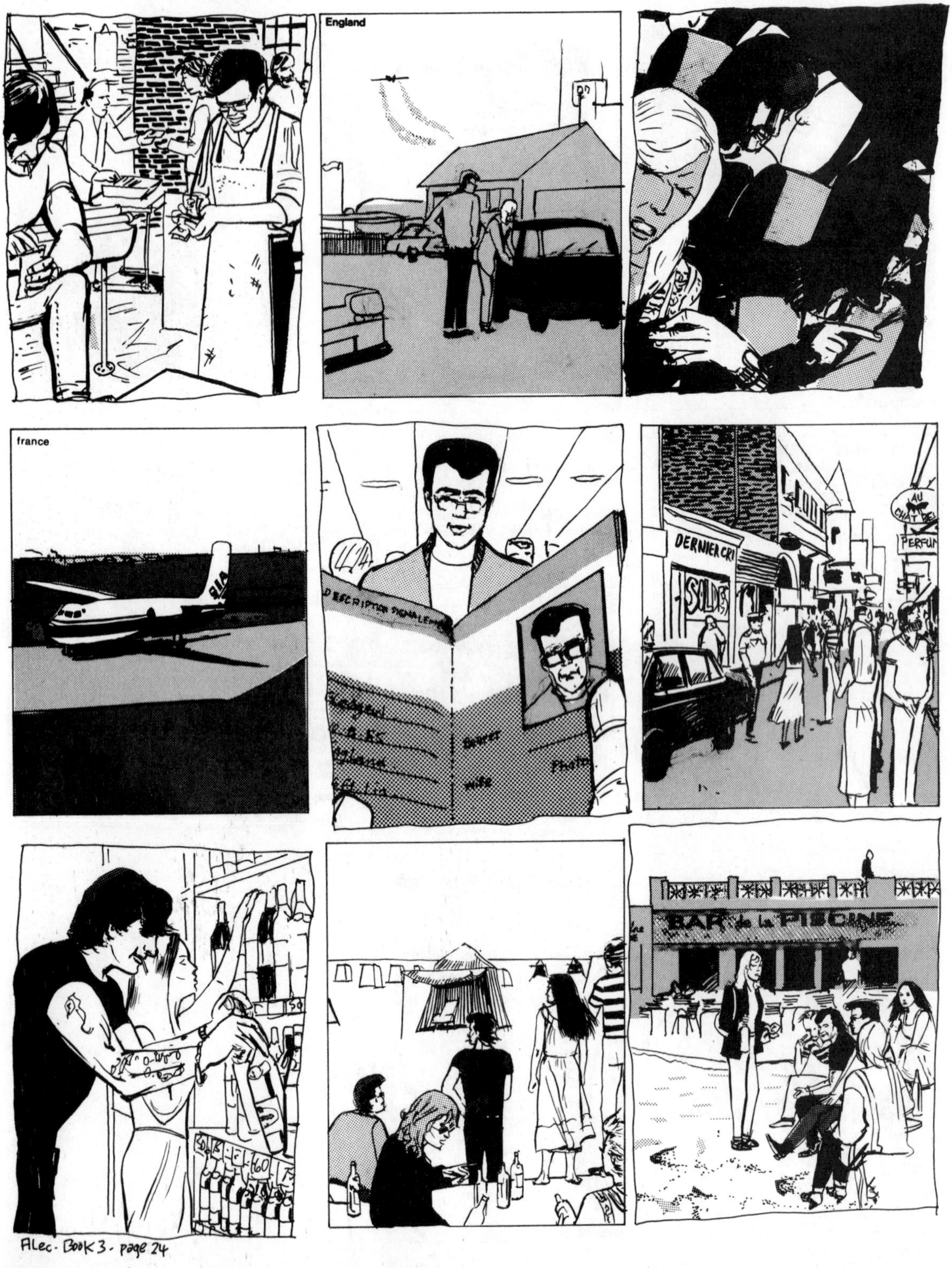
England
france
DERNIER CRI
SOLDES
BAR de la PISCINE

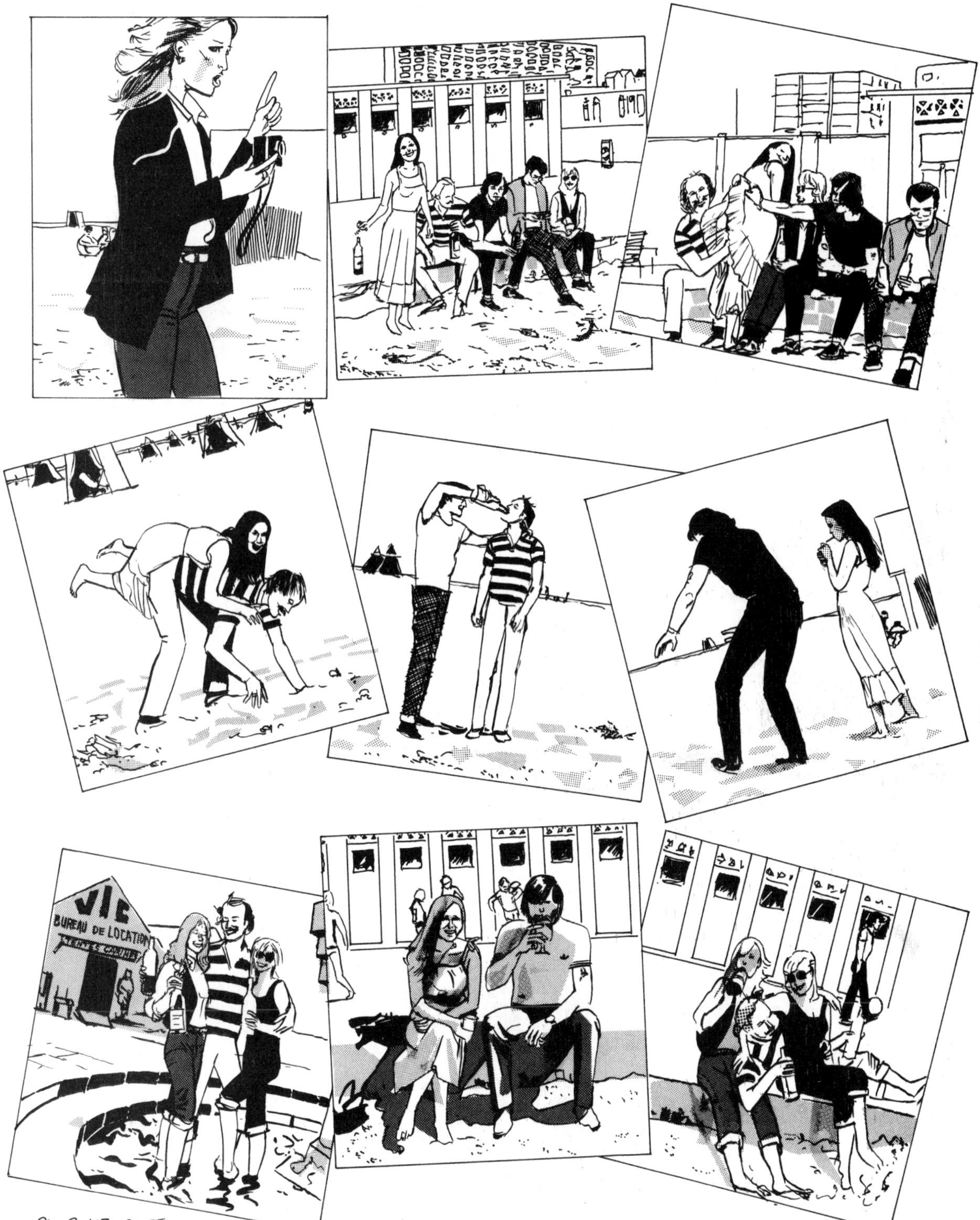
VIC
BUREAU DE LOCATION

ANAïS NIN IN 1946, WRITING IN HER DIARY ABOUT AN AMERICAN SUBURB WHILE LONGING FOR FRANCE —

" EVERYONE WAS AT HOME WITH BOTTLES FROM WHICH THEY HOPED TO EXTRACT A gaiety bottled ELSEWHERE "

A BIG FISH GIVES ME THE EVIL EYE

I THOUGHT I WAS IN A COLD SWEAT BUT IN FACT MY JEANS ARE STILL SATURATED WITH SEAWATER.

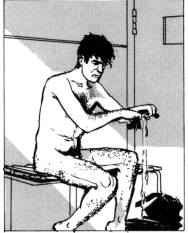

I'M BACK IN THE VICIOUS DROWNING DREAM. I GO OVER IT IN MY CONSCIOUS MIND. I'M BACK IN GLASGOW WHERE ALL OF MY DREAMS PARTLY HAPPEN.

I GO THROUGH AN ENGLAND KITCHEN DOOR INTO A SCOTLAND SITTING ROOM IN MY COMPOSITE DREAMHOUSE. I GET IN A STAGECOACH.

I PASS A HOUSE I USED TO PASS AS A CHILD ON MY WAY TO SCHOOL, WHEN THE POSTMAN WOULD INVITE ME TO WALK UNDER HIS CAPE OUT OF THE RAIN.

I REMEMBER A BIG DOG WAS ALWAYS AT THE WINDOW, WATCHING ME GO OFF DOWN THE ROAD OF MY LIFE.

I HAVE OFTEN EXPECTED TO SEE HIM EVEN NOW, AT OTHER WINDOWS.

I'M WITH ELIZABETH BONNATTI MY CHILDHOOD SWEETHEART, SHOWING OFF JUST BEFORE A MATCH.

THOSE MATCHES — I REMEMBER THE WHOLE TEAM, IN LINES AND STANZAS (FILL IN YOUR OWN ELEVEN).

PETER HUDDLESTON WITH HIS PUDDING BOWL RAZORED HAIRCUT. JIM IRELAND PUSHING THEM OUT DEPENDABLY.

HUGH MacDONALD, MY BOSOM PAL, WAS CAPTAIN AND LATER, IT IS SAID, A PRIEST.

JOHNNY MURPHY, PADDY DOYLE ME, CENTRE-FORWARD, COMPLETELY IN THE WRONG PLACE, BUT INTUITIVELY RIGHT FOR THE MOST INGENIOUS SHOT AGAINST THE BRICKWALLS.

THE THOMASSOS WERE CLAPPING THEIR HANDS OFF.

AH ME, I WAKE UP IN MY LITTLE ROOM IN SOUTHEND.

ALEC. BOOK 3 · page 28

NOPE, I'M STILL HERE.

THEY'VE THROWN A DONKEY JACKET OVER ME.

THE MOST EXQUISITE DONKEY JACKET. IT HAS A LORRY CAB AROMA OF CHEERFULLY MUNDANE CARDBOARD BOX DELIVERIES.

ALTHOUGH I HAVE THAT THING ONLY A FEW HOURS IT'S ONE OF THE MOST AGREEABLE COATS I HAVE POSSESSED.

IT'S THE ONLY STIMULUS IN THIS PLACE, BECAUSE THE WINDOWS ARE OF A FROSTED GLASS DESIGN...

...SHOWING A NEAT UNDERSTANDING OF DETENTION AS PUNISHMENT.

IF I COULD SEE KIDS IN THE STREET OR PIGEONS ON THE SLATES I COULD BE CONTENT FOR A WHILE. I CAN'T EVEN SEE TOO WELL WITHOUT MY GLASSES.

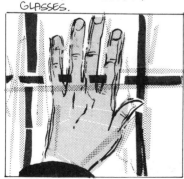

I TRY TO DREAM AGAIN BUT I'VE RUN OUT OF SLEEP.

HAVE THEY LOCKED ME UP FOR A GAG OR DO THEY SERIOUSLY REGARD ME AS A MENACE TO FAMILY BATHING?

I NOTICE MY CLOTHES ARE SPREAD OVER A RADIATOR.

THE NEXT HOUR (TWO? FOUR?) IS PAINFUL. EITHER THE SUN'S OVER THE OTHER SIDE OF THE BUILDING OR IT'S GETTING LATE. MAYBE I'VE MISSED THE PLANE HOME.

IT DAWNS ON ME THAT PENNY HAS MY PASSPORT IN HER HANDBAG AND IF I DON'T GET TO THE AIRPORT BY SEVEN I'LL BE IN AN EVEN BIGGER FIX.

SOON AS I GET OUT OF THERE AGG THE RADIATORS AREN'T ON.!!

OH DAMNIT! ANYWAY THE BOOTS ARE ON

I'M A BIG GUY AGAIN — NOBODY'S GONNA STEP ON MY SKELETON FEET.

I'LL MARCH ACROSS EUROPE.

LOSE MYSELF IN A THOUSAND ADVENTURES.

PENNY IS PEEVED.

THE FISH IS INTACT.

THERE'S NO PLANE BACK.
REPLACEMENT TRANSPORT IS
PROVIDED ONLY AFTER PROTEST.

GEORGE IS UNRULY.

HIS CLUB MEMBERSHIP
IS LATER SUSPENDED

DANNY SMUGGLES THE COD
ONTO THE FERRY.

HE HAD HALF A PLAN TO TAKE
IT TO AUNT LUCY'S PARTY.

DANNY MOVES INTO A FLAT
WITH HOLLY.

THEY GET MARRIED A FEW
MONTHS LATER.

ALEC · BOOK 3 · PAGE 31

AS FOR ALL THIS DROWNING STUFF. I FELL IN THE THAMES WHILE STANDING UP IN GEORGE WAITE'S DINGHY.

I LIED EARLIER ABOUT THE FUNNY NOTIONS,

IN FACT THE IMAGINATION MUST CEASE TO FUNCTION—

ONE MUST BECOME MACHINE-LIKE

.., AUTOMATIC.

~ chomp! ~

ARE YOU COMING TO BED EARLY TONIGHT? - YOU CAN DO THOSE LAST THREE PICTURES TOMORROW—

YEH.. ANYWAY THERE'S NOTHING MORE TO SAY—

chookie chicken !!

TRIO IN AN IMPROMPTU PUB SINGSONG EASTER SUNDAY, BRIGHTON, 1986 ~.

— Eddie Campbell —

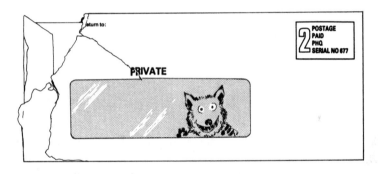

Return to:

POSTAGE
PAID
PHQ
SERIAL NO 677

PRIVATE

BOOK FOUR

ALAS POOR ALEC

ONE NIGHT SIX YEARS AFTER THE END OF THIS BOOK, DANNY GREY GETS THE TWO OF US INTO A FIGHT.

WHICH DOESN'T HAVE ANY OF THE BALLETIC PERFECTION OF THE GATOR'S RUMPUS. INDEED, A YOUNG TURK WIPES THE FLOOR WITH OUR BOY.

DANNY SMOULDERS FOR AN HOUR THEN DISAPPEARS BACK TO THE SCENE OF THE INCIDENT.

ON HIS RETURN, HE AND HOLLY HIGH-TAIL IT OUT OF THE TOWN WHERE I'M LIVING. SHE LATER TELLS ME A SCREW DRIVER IS MISSING FROM THE TOOL BOX.

DANNY CAN REMEMBER NOTHING ABOUT IT, AND THIS BUSINESS LINGERS IN MY MIND AS A DISQUIETING EXAMPLE OF HIS FIERCE VANITY...

...ONE OF THE MAN'S DARKER CORNERS THAT BECAME REVEALED TO ME NEAR THE END OF THE KING CANUTE DAYS.

THERE WERE NIGHTS BACK THEN WHEN WE HAD LOUD DISAGREEMENTS

I never won sherry in any raffle — I remember these things

You're a supercilious bastard!!

AND TIMES ON THE WORKING HIGHWAY WHEN HIS TEMPER EXPLODED.

I'll fukkin' teach you to make signs at me!!

WAIT!

..I'm only trying to tell you that you've been dropping your load for two miles!!

oh my God

I PREFER TO REMEMBER OTHER TIMES, DIFFERENT ENTIRELY MOMENTS OF CHILDLIKE WONDER- A LOVE OF SIMPLE THINGS.

EVEN WHEN HE'S NOT IN THE PICTURE, HE'S THE TOUCHSTONE FOR THE SPECIAL GAEITY OF THE KING CANUTE. WITHOUT HIM IT WILL, AND DOES, DISSIPATE.

EVEN AFTER HE MARRIES HOLLY, THE CAVALCADE OF INCIDENTS AND ADVENTURES CONTINUES.

WHEN HE INHERITS SOME MONEY (TO COME) HE WASTES IT IN A GRAND AND MEMORABLE STYLE.

AND IN THE MEANTIME, WHEN PAYDAY IS SLOW IN COMING, THERE IS THAT SUBTERRANEAN ECONOMICS.

A LARGE DRUM OF DIESEL MIGHT GO MISSING AND BE SOLD TO FINANCE HIS EVENING AT THE CANUTE,

OR GETTING AWAY FROM MONEY AND PROFIT ALTOGETHER TOWARDS A MORE PERFECT BALANCE OF EXCHANGES WHERE ONLY PROVIDENCE KEEPS THE BOOKS.

WHERE ONE GUY MIGHT HAVE A LOAD OF BROKEN CONCRETE TO GET RID OF FROM HIS HOUSE RENOVATIONS AND DANNY GREY CHEERFULLY ASSISTS

THEN ANOTHER GUY WILL IMMEDIATELY ANNOUNCE HIS NEED OF 'CRAZY PAVING' FOR HIS FRONT GARDEN.

THERE WAS A COUPLE WHO LIVED NEAR THE KING CANUTE – SHEP AND JEAN – WE SPENT A WHOLE SUMMER CONVENING IN THEIR HOUSE AFTER PUB-CLOSING.

uh.. I've just moved in daorwoon the road and I've got this concrete to shift

WITH BEER FROM THE PUB, AND WE'D TALK AND SING AND DANCE TILL LATE AND SLEEP ON THE FLOOR TILL MORNING.

THEY HAD COME FROM BUCKINGHAMSHIRE AND TOOK US BACK THAT WAY ON THREE OCCASIONS TO A SMALL COUNTRY PLACE WHOSE NAME I FORGET (IT WAS ON ONE OF THESE JAUNTS THAT I FELL IN THE RIVER).

WE'D SLEEP ON THE BACK OF THE TRUCK OUTSIDE THIS PICTURESQUE PUB – THE LANDLORD'S NAME WAS BERT.

It was a hot foggy day in Julember

ON ONE OCCASION LITTLE PAULINE WAS WITH US AND BERT HAD GIVEN ME AND PENNY A SMALL UPSTAIRS ROOM FOR THE NIGHT.

IN THE MORNING THE CHILD WOULD NOT SPEAK TO ME AND NATURALLY I FIGURED I'D DONE SOMETHING BAD – BUT

She wet herself in the night. don't say anthing about it.

IT GOT ME THINKING ABOUT THE PECULIAR PHENOMENON OF NOCTURNAL URINARY ADVENTURES, PARTICULARLY WITH REGARD TO DANNY GREY.

DRUNKENNESS WOULD NEVER SHOW ON MY FRIEND BUT HE WOULD GO TO BED CONTENTEDLY AND WAKE UP AN HOUR LATER AS A CRAZED PISSING SOMNAMBULIST.

WARDROBES WOULD BE CAREFULLY LOCKED AND SEALED THE PREVIOUS EVENING BY HIS NEAREST AND DEAREST. ARMCHAIRS WOULD BE CAUTIOUSLY PUSHED AGAINST SIDEBOARD DOORS.

THE FINAL OCCASION THAT WE DROVE THE SEVENTY MILES TO BERT'S PUB WAS TO CELEBRATE HIS RETIREMENT. THAT NIGHT WE WERE SLEEPING IN THE HOUSE OF AMERICAN FRIENDS OF SHEP AND JEAN.

I WAS NOT PRESENT MYSELF AT THE TIME IN QUESTION — HAVING HAD ONE OF MY INCREASINGLY REGULAR FLARE-UPS WITH PENNY MOORE.

I WAS IN FACT SLEEPING IN OUR CAR AFTER STORMING AROUND FOR FOUR HOURS IN THE COUNTRY NIGHT BEFORE DISCOVERING A REMARKABLE, ALMOST SPIRITUAL CALM.

PENNY SAID SHE WAS WAKENED BY THE SOUND OF RAIN ON THE ROOF, BUT ON COCKING HER EAR BECAME DISTURBED BY THE APPARENT NEARNESS OF IT.

SHE SAT BOLT UPRIGHT IN TIME TO SEE DANNY GREY URINATING ON LEN WAITE IN HIS SLEEPING BAG.

THE POOR GUY SLEPT THROUGH IT AND THEY TOLD HIM THE FISH TANK HAD LEAKED.

Pitta patta pitta

Shep! Help!

Heh heh!

Maybe it came out here Roger.

DANNY, OF COURSE, KNEW NOTHING OF THE INCIDENT.

raayoond the raayoondaboot

SPEAKING OF PECULIAR BEHAVIOUR — HERE'S DAVE TIMMINS — I HAD STARTED TO THINK HE WAS BECOMING A BETTER ADJUSTED INDIVIDUAL — AT LEAST, HE HAD STARTED TO GRASP THAT SUBLIME PHILOSOPHY OF THE TRUE WASTER.

It's just the realization that nothing matters — whatever you do is basically pointless.

THAT EVENING, SHEP AND JEAN'S PLACE — THERE WERE MORE THAN 17 PEOPLE INSIDE, SO I WAS OUTSIDE WITH TIMMINS —

Observe, Alec..In light of what we were discussing earlier — this twig which I now put in my wallet ..lateral thinking

Uh- you're broke so your wallet's in a splint

No,No

JUST LIKE THIS, HE STARTS FALLING OVER.

TIMMINS' HUMILITY ISN'T REALISTIC, -WHICH IS NOT TO SAY THAT IT ISN'T REAL- HERE'S PENNY ASKING HIM TO MOVE HER CAR— NOT "BE A DEAR, DAVE, I CAN'T SEEM TO FIND MY SHOES," BUT OUTRIGHT.

SHE RECOGNISED WHAT MUST HAVE BEEN SERVILE TRAITS -IT GRATED WITH ME THAT SHE HAD THE POOR GUY RUNNING AROUND CHIVALROUSLY WHILE AT THE SAME TIME SEEMED ONLY TO HATE HIM BECAUSE OF IT.

THEN SHE'D LOVE HIM FOR SOMETHING ELSE- LIKE HIS BRASH CONFIDENCE IN TELLING FUNNY STORIES -I GUESS THESE THINGS FIND THEIR OWN BALANCE.

BACK TO SHEP AND JEAN, IT'S THE NIGHT OF ONE OF OUR FANCY-DRESS PARTIES AT THE KING CANUTE.

AFTERWARDS JEAN DISAPPEARS INTO THE DARK WANDERING THE STREET IN SEMI-DRESS AND IS PICKED UP BY THE POLICE WHO DELIVER HER HOME.

SHEP UNEXPECTEDLY HAS A FIT OF THUNDEROUS ANGER.

DRINK BRINGS US TOGETHER IN WIT, LAUGHTER, FELLOWSHIP AND PLEASANT FOLLY.

THEN CHURNS UP ALL THE MUDDIER ECSTASIES — THE NOCTURNAL URINARY ADVENTURES, THE FITS OF THUNDEROUS ANGER.

TODAY IF WE WANT WE CAN GET THROUGH OUR LIVES ON A PROSAIC MEAT-AND-TWO-VEG.

OR FROM TIME TO TIME WE CAN PARTAKE OF SOME SWEET COMMUNAL POETIC FRUIT.

get dawloon shep

AND RISK FLEXING THE DARKENED MUSCLES OF OUR PSYCHOLOGICAL BACK-PASSAGE — DO A BEHAVIOURAL POOPOO, SO TO SPEAK.

I BUMPED INTO TIMMINS A COUPLE OF YEARS AFTER THE KING CANUTE PERIOD. HE WAS A BOUNCER AT A CLUB DOOR. OR APPEARED TO BE.

Hello Alec.

HE PULLED ME IN FOR A BEER.

I'll never forgive Danny. He played me for a fool

SAID HE WAS ACTUALLY ON A WEEKEND OFF FROM THE ARMY AND THAT HE WAS HOPEFULLY OFF TO THE FALKLANDS WAR NEXT WEEK — SO THERE YOU GO.

ONE MORE OF SHEP'S BELLY BUTTON THEN PRETEND YOU'RE AT THE MOVIES.

snowr

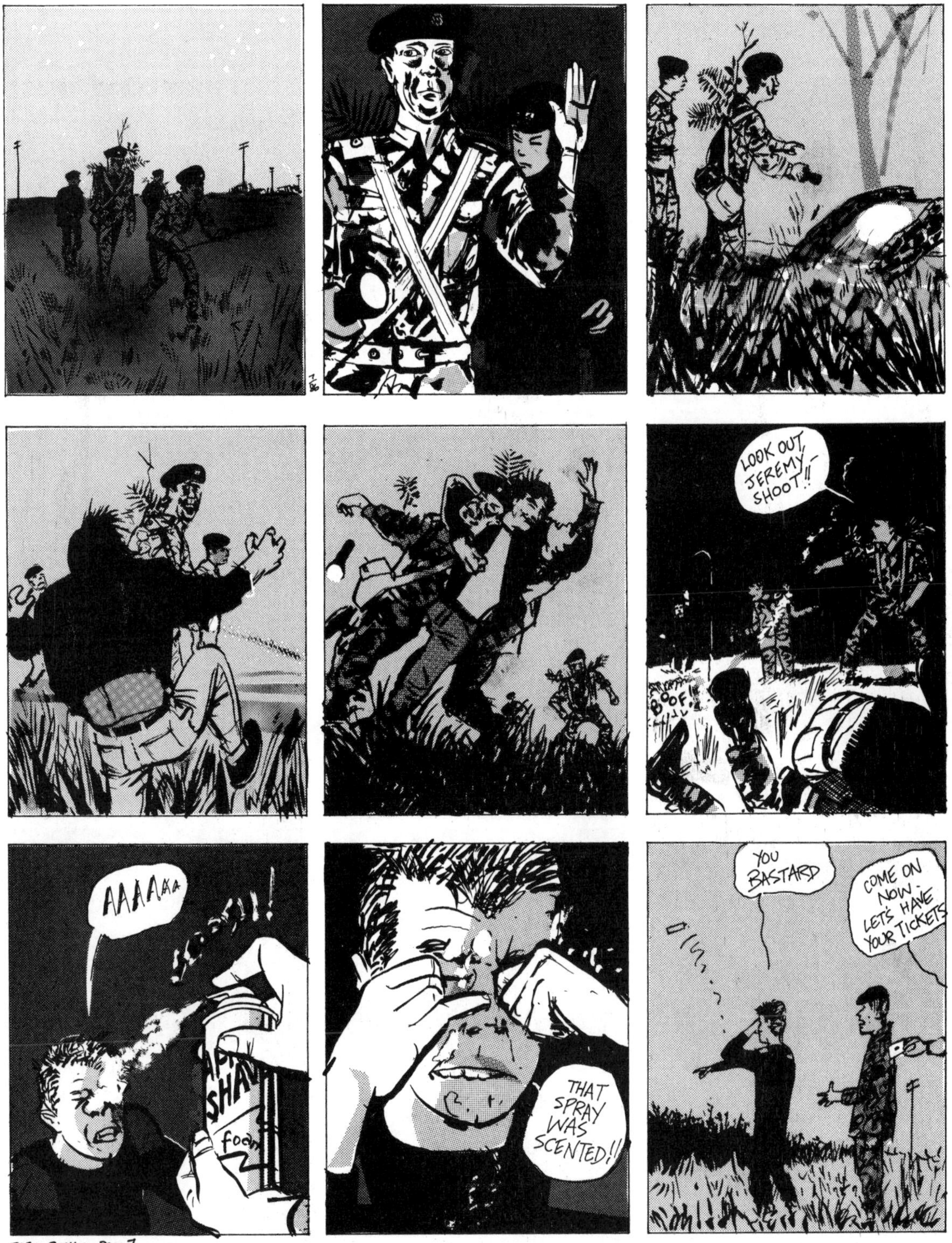
7/86
LOOK OUT, JEREMY - SHOOT!!
BOOF!!
AAAAAA
THAT SPRAY WAS SCENTED!!
YOU BASTARD
COME ON NOW - LETS HAVE YOUR TICKETS

ALEC. BOOK 4. Page 7

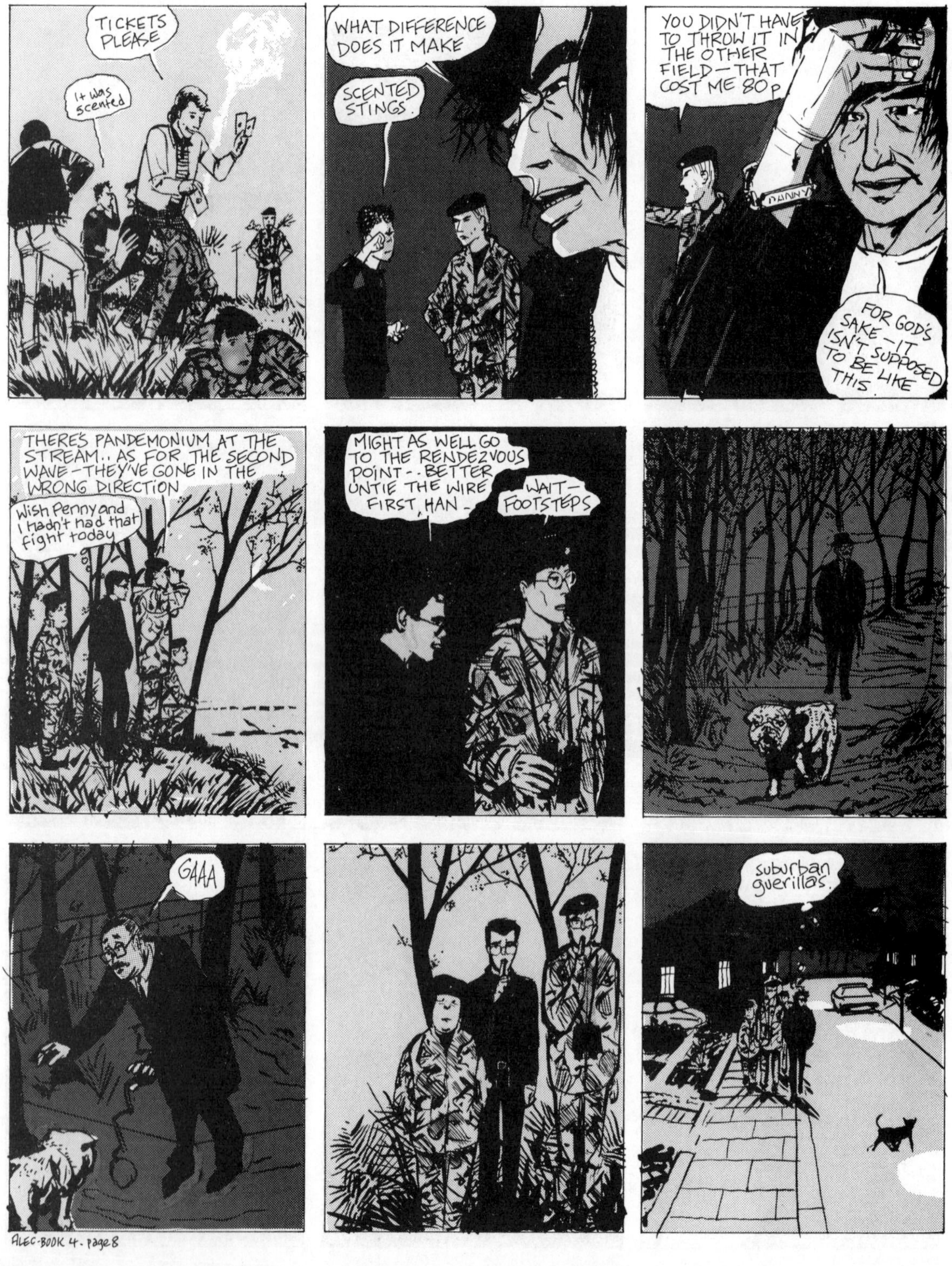
TICKETS PLEASE
It was scented
WHAT DIFFERENCE DOES IT MAKE
SCENTED STINGS.
YOU DIDN'T HAVE TO THROW IT IN THE OTHER FIELD—THAT COST ME 80p
DANNY
FOR GOD'S SAKE—IT ISN'T SUPPOSED TO BE LIKE THIS.
THERE'S PANDEMONIUM AT THE STREAM.. AS FOR THE SECOND WAVE—THEY'VE GONE IN THE WRONG DIRECTION
Wish Penny and I hadn't had that fight today
MIGHT AS WELL GO TO THE RENDEZVOUS POINT-. BETTER UNTIE THE WIRE FIRST, HAN.
WAIT— FOOTSTEPS
GAAA
suburban guerillas.

MUST Phone Penny

IT'S BEEN REALLY GOOD SO FAR—WE STAGED A BATTLE MANOEUVRE TONIGHT —

WELL, THE MEN FROM THE PUB ARRANGED IT REALLY...THEY PHOTOCOPIED A MAP AND THEY HID IN THE WOODS, AND SOME OF US WENT WITH THEM AND THE REST OF US HAD TO GET THROUGH

TO REACH THE MOUND ON THE HILL ....WE'RE BACK AT BASE NOW AND WE'RE JUST ABOUT TO HAVE SOME SOUP AND BED DOWN FOR THE NIGHT.. YES, UH, DAD? — YES, PUT HIM ON,

HELLO, DAD—YES, WELL THE MEN FROM THE PUB ARRANGED IT ALL..THEY PHOTOCOPIED MAPS AND THEY HID IN THE WOODS., SOME OF US WENT WITH THEM AND THE REST HAD TO GET

THROUGH..WE'RE BACK AT BASE AND WE'RE JUST GOING TO HAVE SOME SOUP AND BED DOWN FOR THE NIGHT... YES ..HELLO .. MUM !! IS THAT YOU.. YES... WELL THE MEN FROM THE PUB

THEY HID IN THE WOODS AND THE REST OF US HAD TO GET THROUGH ...NO .. IT WASN'T DANGEROUS.

WE'RE BACK AT BASE CAMP AND WE'RE JUST ABOUT TO HAVE SOME SOUP AND BED DOWN FOR THE NIGHT.

EH ? ... UM ... OXTAIL.

ALEC · BOOK 4 · page 9

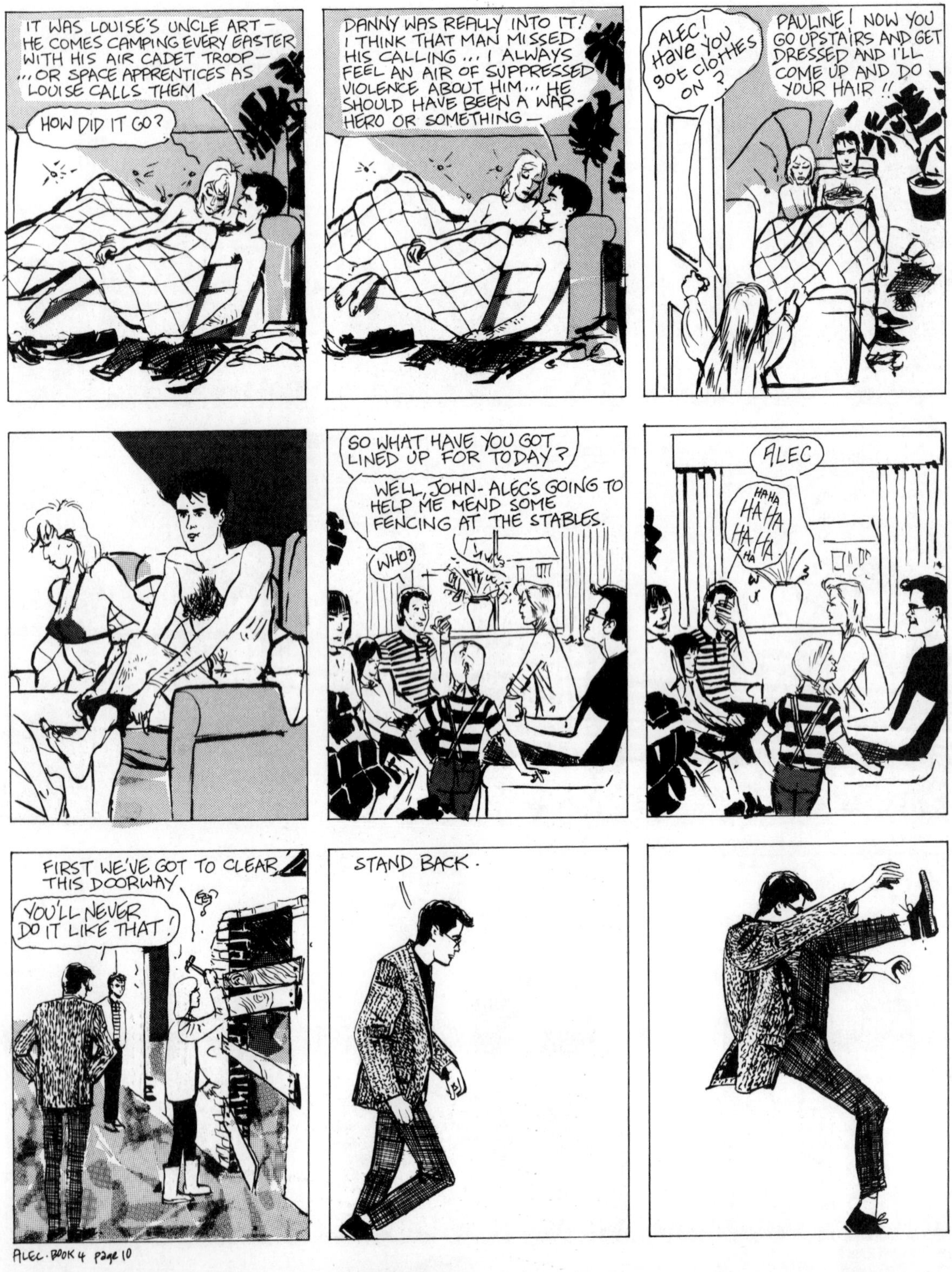
IT WAS LOUISE'S UNCLE ART – HE COMES CAMPING EVERY EASTER WITH HIS AIR CADET TROOP – ...OR SPACE APPRENTICES AS LOUISE CALLS THEM
HOW DID IT GO?
DANNY WAS REALLY INTO IT! I THINK THAT MAN MISSED HIS CALLING ... I ALWAYS FEEL AN AIR OF SUPPRESSED VIOLENCE ABOUT HIM... HE SHOULD HAVE BEEN A WAR-HERO OR SOMETHING –
ALEC! Have you got clothes on?
PAULINE! NOW YOU GO UPSTAIRS AND GET DRESSED AND I'LL COME UP AND DO YOUR HAIR!!
SO WHAT HAVE YOU GOT LINED UP FOR TODAY?
WELL, JOHN - ALEC'S GOING TO HELP ME MEND SOME FENCING AT THE STABLES.
WHO?
ALEC
HA HA HA HA HA HA HA HA
FIRST WE'VE GOT TO CLEAR THIS DOORWAY
YOU'LL NEVER DO IT LIKE THAT!
STAND BACK.

The Horrid Vision in the Shaving Mirror

A short story in six pictures having nothing to do with any of the previous stuff –

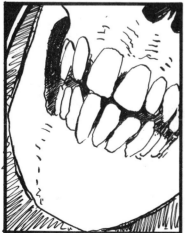

THIS IS WHERE I WORK.

GOGGLES MUST BE WORN

I CUT SHEET-METAL INTO RECTANGLES TO MAKE DUCTING AND PIPE.

THE HEAVIEST METAL I HANDLE IS 18 gauge WHICH IS NO BIG DEAL, BUT LUGGING 9-foot SHEETS AROUND KEEPS ME FIT.

AT THE OTHER END THERE'S 28 gauge - THE GUYS HERE SAY YOU CAN WRAP YOUR SANDWICHES IN IT. THAT'S THEIR LITTLE JOKE. WITH A LONG RUN OF THIS I'LL SHRED ONE PAIR OF GLOVES PER DAY.

BUT I LIKE THOSE LONG RUNS. THE BIGGER THE ORDER, THE MORE REPETITIVE MY JOB IS AND I CAN FREE MY BRAIN FOR OTHER THINGS.

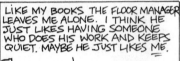

LIKE MY BOOKS THE FLOOR MANAGER LEAVES ME ALONE. I THINK HE JUST LIKES HAVING SOMEONE WHO DOES HIS WORK AND KEEPS QUIET. MAYBE HE JUST LIKES ME.

STOP LOAFING!

BUT LOOK AT HIM! HE'S READING BOOKS

I'M TALKING ABOUT YOU, NOT HIM

ANYWAY, I'VE GOT A RARE PILE OF CHOSEN VOLUMES BACK HERE. HERE'S A FAVOURITE :- *THE GREEK MYTHS*, by ROBERT GRAVES.

THIS BOOK DRAWS HEAVILY ON A VERY INTERESTING PROPOSITION - THE THEORY THAT EARLIEST HUMAN SOCIETY HAD AN ENTIRELY MATRIARCHAL BASIS.

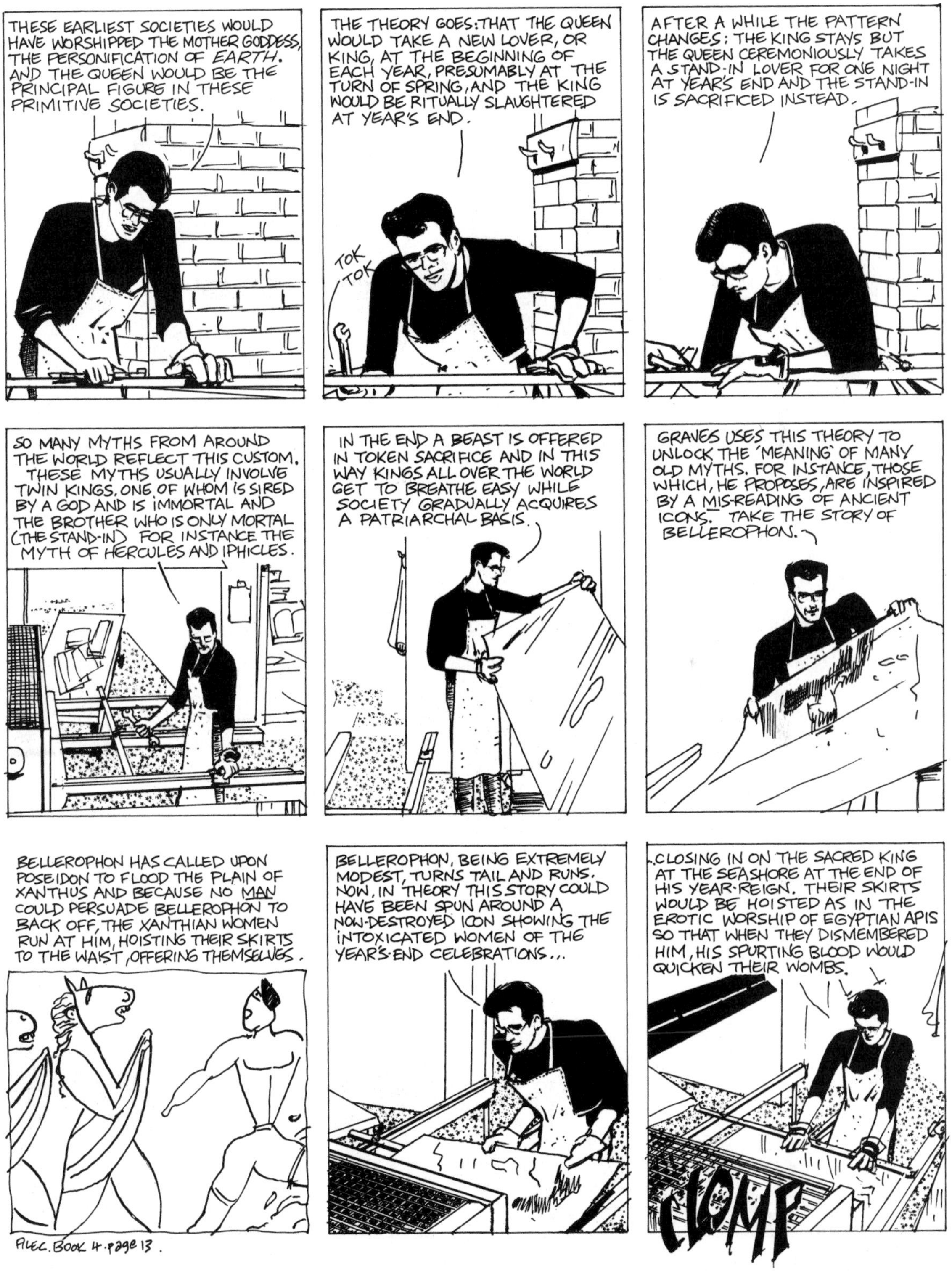
THESE EARLIEST SOCIETIES WOULD HAVE WORSHIPPED THE MOTHER GODDESS, THE PERSONIFICATION OF *EARTH*. AND THE QUEEN WOULD BE THE PRINCIPAL FIGURE IN THESE PRIMITIVE SOCIETIES.
THE THEORY GOES: THAT THE QUEEN WOULD TAKE A NEW LOVER, OR KING, AT THE BEGINNING OF EACH YEAR, PRESUMABLY AT THE TURN OF SPRING, AND THE KING WOULD BE RITUALLY SLAUGHTERED AT YEAR'S END.
TOK TOK
AFTER A WHILE THE PATTERN CHANGES: THE KING STAYS BUT THE QUEEN CEREMONIOUSLY TAKES A STAND-IN LOVER FOR ONE NIGHT AT YEAR'S END AND THE STAND-IN IS SACRIFICED INSTEAD.
SO MANY MYTHS FROM AROUND THE WORLD REFLECT THIS CUSTOM. THESE MYTHS USUALLY INVOLVE TWIN KINGS, ONE OF WHOM IS SIRED BY A GOD AND IS IMMORTAL AND THE BROTHER WHO IS ONLY MORTAL (THE STAND-IN) FOR INSTANCE THE MYTH OF HERCULES AND IPHICLES.
IN THE END A BEAST IS OFFERED IN TOKEN SACRIFICE AND IN THIS WAY KINGS ALL OVER THE WORLD GET TO BREATHE EASY WHILE SOCIETY GRADUALLY ACQUIRES A PATRIARCHAL BASIS.
GRAVES USES THIS THEORY TO UNLOCK THE 'MEANING' OF MANY OLD MYTHS. FOR INSTANCE, THOSE WHICH, HE PROPOSES, ARE INSPIRED BY A MIS-READING OF ANCIENT ICONS. TAKE THE STORY OF BELLEROPHON.
BELLEROPHON HAS CALLED UPON POSEIDON TO FLOOD THE PLAIN OF XANTHUS AND BECAUSE NO MAN COULD PERSUADE BELLEROPHON TO BACK OFF, THE XANTHIAN WOMEN RUN AT HIM, HOISTING THEIR SKIRTS TO THE WAIST, OFFERING THEMSELVES.
BELLEROPHON, BEING EXTREMELY MODEST, TURNS TAIL AND RUNS. NOW, IN THEORY THIS STORY COULD HAVE BEEN SPUN AROUND A NOW-DESTROYED ICON SHOWING THE INTOXICATED WOMEN OF THE YEAR'S-END CELEBRATIONS...
..CLOSING IN ON THE SACRED KING AT THE SEASHORE AT THE END OF HIS YEAR-REIGN. THEIR SKIRTS WOULD BE HOISTED AS IN THE EROTIC WORSHIP OF EGYPTIAN APIS SO THAT WHEN THEY DISMEMBERED HIM, HIS SPURTING BLOOD WOULD QUICKEN THEIR WOMBS.
CLOMF

ALEC. BOOK 4. page 13.

DEFINITELY IN MY ALL-TIME *TOP FIVE*. BUT SOME TIME LATER I WAS BROWSING IN A BIOGRAPHY OF GRAVES AND A LINE JUMPED OUT AT ME, A LINE WHICH REMARKED ON GRAVES' SUPPORT OF THE "ANTHROPOLOGICALLY UNTENABLE THEORY OF THE MATRIARCHAL BASIS OF EARLIEST HUMAN SOCIETY"

CLOMP

HERE'S ONE THAT CLEARED AWAY A FEW COBWEBS WHEN I FIRST READ IT: A 1939 *PELICAN EDITION* I PICKED UP FOR 10p IN A JUNK SHOP, *THINKING TO SOME PURPOSE* by L. SUSAN STEBBING.

"ANYONE WHO HOLDS THE BELIEF FIRST AND RATIONALISES IT AFTERWARDS IS PREJUDICED"

I'VE MARKED A FEW LITTLE GEMS. I CALL THEM STEBBING-STONES.

HERE'S ANOTHER :- "OUR NEED TO HAVE DEFINITE BELIEFS TO HOLD ONTO IS GREAT. THE DIFFICULTY OF MASTERING THE EVIDENCE, ON WHICH SUCH BELIEFS OUGHT TO BE BASED, IS BURDENSOME"

ONE LAST ONE.- "THE DIVERGENCE BETWEEN MY INTERESTS AND YOURS MAY LEAD ME TO USE AN ARGUMENT THE FORCE OF WHICH I SHOULD BE UNABLE TO RECOGNISE WERE OUR POSITIONS REVERSED."

I DON'T READ A LOT OF NOVELS, I MUST CONFESS. IN FACT AS A RACE WE DON'T READ A LOT OF FICTION ANYMORE, AS OPPOSED TO DICKENS' TIME WHEN THE PUBLIC WERE BUYING *OLIVER TWIST* IN NUMBERS THAT SOME OF OUR NATIONAL NEWSPAPERS WOULD BE HAPPY WITH.

THIS IS JOSEPH HELLER'S *SOMETHING HAPPENED* - HIS SECOND NOVEL, FOLLOWING THE FAMOUS *CATCH 22*, WHICH I ACTUALLY HAD TROUBLE GETTING THROUGH. BUT THIS ONE . I GUESS IT'S FOR THE ENTIRELY SELFISH REASON THAT I IDENTIFY WITH SO MUCH OF IT.

"GERALDINE WAS NOT AS SMART AS I WAS BUT WAS GOING ALL THE WAY ALREADY WITH GUYS AS OLD AND AS BIG AS MY BIG BROTHER, WHILE I WASN'T EVEN JERKING OFF YET."

LATER, THIS BIT.."PRETTY AS SHE WAS, SHE COULD TURN AS GRISLY TO ME ALL AT ONCE AS THAT SEPARATED HEAD OF MEDUSA, THAT EVIL, HAIRY, PERISTALTIC NEST OF COUNTLESS CRAWLING

VIPERS ARCHING OUT TO FANG ME."

HI ALEC

HOW'S IT GOIN', DANNY. Y'KNOW, I'M DEEP IN THIS BOOK HERE, I KEEP SEEING MY RELATIONSHIP WITH PENNY IN IT.

YEH, HEY, I'VE GOT AN IDEA —

LIKE THIS BIT.."PRETTY AS SHE WAS..

FOR HEAVEN'S SAKE!! YOU READ ALL THESE BOOKS AND YOU SEE PENNY IN THEM ALL!!

THEY WROTE ALL THOSE BOOKS JUST FOR YOU AND PENNY. PENNY, PENNY, YOU'RE BESOTTED WITH THE GIRL, YOU'VE GOT NO TIME FOR ANYONE ELSE SINCE PENNY!!!

I WAS GOING TO SAY LET'S GO OUT FOR A DRINK, BUT YOU WOULDN'T COME, WOULD YOU?!"

NOW!!? BLOODY NO, I WOULDN'T —

F —

AH!

"IT HIT ME WITH THE FORCE OF A FUTURE RECOLLECTION." THATS FROM NABOKOV'S *LOLITA*

IS THAT A BOOK?

YOU ONLY KNOW BOOKS. YOU DON'T KNOW ANYTHING FOR YOURSELF, DO YOU? WHY DON'T YOU GO OUT AND LEARN SOMETHING FOR YOURSELF? EH?

ALEC. BOOK 4. PAGE 15

HERE I AM MURDERING PENNY MOORE IN A GUEST HOUSE IN A DREAM.

YOU WILL UNDERSTAND, OF COURSE, THAT I AM OBSESSED WITH THE GIRL.

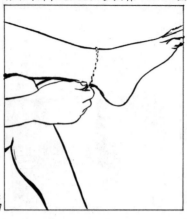

WHEN WITH FRIENDS I WILL OFTEN WATCH HER ATTENTIVELY. I'LL STARE EVEN. I'LL MAKE EVERYONE FEEL UNCOMFORTABLE.

I ONLY MENTION THIS IN CASE YOU ARE IN SOME FAR FLUNG ILLITERATE FUTURE WHERE MY POOR LITTLE BOOK IS THE TEXT IN YOUR ENGLISH LIT. GRADUATION EXAM. I SHOULD WANT YOU TO HAVE ALL THE INFORMATION AT YOUR DISPOSAL.

YOU MIGHT TRY SAYING THAT ALEC MacGARRY IS OVERSENSITIVE TO SENSATIONS OF THE INEVITABILITY OF AGE AND DECLINE.

YOU MIGHT WANT TO POSTULATE THAT HE SUFFERS FROM THE NORMAL INSECURITY OF WANTING TO BE WITH THE PERFECT WOMAN BECAUSE THAT WOULD INDICATE THE MEASURE OF HIS MANHOOD.

HE MIGHT UNDER THOSE CONDITIONS ATTACH UNDUE SIGNIFICANCE TO PENNY MOORE'S TWO MISSING TEETH FROM HER CAR CRASH LAST YEAR.

YOU UNDOUBTEDLY WILL WISH TO DRAW PARALLELS WITH THE GREAT LITERATURE OF THE PAST.

SO YOU'LL NOTICE I'VE DRAWN A GROSSLY PRETENTIOUS REFERENCE TO SHAKESPEARE UNDER ALL THIS CRAP. HE'S BEEN DEAD SO LONG I DON'T NEED HIS PERMISSION.

WHAT DO WE LEAVE AFTER WE GO? A FEW DULL AND CHIPPED ARTEFACTS?
HERE'S A SCENE AFTER JOHN GODFREY'S BROTHER-IN-LAW COMES INTO THE
PUB CARRYING HIS METAL-DETECTOR. HE'S STILL ON THE TRAIL OF THE
REAL KING CANUTE.

OR PERHAPS SOME EERIE SPIRITUAL
AFTER-EFFECT; AUNT LUCY IS THE
MOST SUPERSTITIOUS PERSON I KNOW;
THIS IS A MONDAY, THE NIGHT AFTER
WE GET BACK FROM LETOUQUET.

SHE'S AT THE PUB THAT NIGHT EN
ROUTE TO LOOKING AT AN UNATTENDED
HOUSE WHICH SHE IS CONSIDERING
BUYING. NATURALLY WE ALL GO
ALONG TO OFFER OUR PROFESSIONAL
OPINIONS AS REALTORS.

THE OMENS, HOWEVER, ARE NOT
GOOD. ORION IS IN THE
CONFLUENCE OF MICKEY MOUSE
AND PLUTO IS IN A TIFF.

SOMEBODY COMMITS THE
CALAMITOUS ERROR OF LIGHTING
A CANDLE WHOSE COLOUR IS THE
PORTENTOUS COLOUR GREEN.

FURTHERMORE, SHEP, WHO IS BY
TRADE A PLUMBER, FINDS SEVERAL
LENGTHS OF COPPER PIPE IN THE
HALL AND BLOWS DOWN ONE OF THEM.

ALEC-BOOK 4-PAGE 17

AUNT LUCY THROWS A FANCY DRESS PARTY. THE THEME IS INDIA. MAKE OF THIS PICTURE WHAT YOU WILL.

LUCY, IN FACT, WAS BORN AND GREW UP IN INDIA IN THE TIME WHEN IT WAS STILL UNDER ENGLISH RULE. SHE TELLS A RATHER TOUCHING STORY ABOUT WHEN SHE WAS A CHILD AND HER LITTLE DOG DIED.

IN 1920's INDIA NOBODY IS LIKELY TO WEEP MUCH OVER A POOR DEAD DOG, BUT A LITTLE SERVANT BOY INTUITIVELY IMPROVISES A FUNERAL PROCESSION AND MOCK BURIAL.

LUCY, LIKE TIMMINS, IS NOT A GREAT FAN OF DANNY GREY AT THIS TIME, FOR REASONS MADE OBVIOUS SOME PAGES BACK. INDEED, ANGELINE WAS QUITE HEARTBROKEN FOR A WHILE.

LUCY'S O.K BY ME. I'LL EVEN FORGIVE THIS SINCE IT IS QUITE TRUE.

ALEC? - WHAT FUTURE DOES HE HAVE - HE HASN'T GOT A TRADE - YOU HAVE LITTLE PAULINE TO THINK OF.

SHEP AND JEAN SEEM TO FALL OUT WITH DANNY TOO. BUT I DON'T KNOW WHY FOR SURE. JEAN IS QUITE PARANOID AFTER SHEP'S FIT OF DOMESTIC VIOLENCE.

NOW THERE'S A GREATLY MISUSED WORD. *PARANOID.* IN COMMON CURRENCY IT MEANS JUST ABOUT ANY SORT OF DISQUIET OR MENTAL DISCOMFORT.

He said the wrong thing to Penny and he's paranoid about it.

HERE'S ANOTHER: PEOPLE SAY *ENORMITY* WHEN THEY MEAN *ENORMOUSNESS.* IT'S A LIVE LANGUAGE, SO WE CAN DEFORM IT AS MUCH AS WE LIKE. DICTIONARIES WILL IN THE END SIDE WITH THE MAJORITY, AND IN THIS CASE THEY ALREADY GIVE THE WORDS AS INTERCHANGEABLE.

and that is the real enormity, your honour.

ON THE OTHER HAND, LATIN, BEING A DEAD LANGUAGE, IS FOREVER PERFECT.

nil sine labore MacGarry, that does not mean NO SIGN OF WORK!

HERE'S THE SLIPPERY SLOPE TO THE LAST PAGE. DANNY GREY INHERITS A BIT OF MONEY.

THE OLD BOY FINALLY DIED, MY GRANDMOTHER'S SECOND HUSBAND. SO MY BROTHER AND I GET THE BUNGALOW.

"IT WAS SOLD OFF PRETTY QUICKLY 15 THOU. WE ARRANGED WITH THE ESTATE AGENT TO GET FIVE OF THAT CASH-IN-HAND BECAUSE WE THOUGHT THAT WOULD LET US OUT TAX-WISE."

I HOPE THIS ISN'T GOING TO AFFECT OUR RELATIONSHIP, ME HAVING A BIT OF MONEY.

WELL, I KNOW I WON'T BE TALKING TO YOU AGAIN.

I'LL TELL YOU WHAT! TWO WEEKS FROM NOW WE'LL ALL GO UP TO HARWICH..DO ALL THE PUBS, STAY THE NIGHT.

ACCORDING TO DANNY, HARWICH HAS THE GREATEST CONCENTRATION OF PUBS PER SQUARE MILE IN ALL OF BRITAIN.

ME, HOLLY, YOU AND PENNY, GEORGE AND VICKI.

TWO DAYS BEFORE WE GO TO HARWICH. IT'S THE EASTER SCHOOL HOLIDAY AND THE GUY IN CHARGE OF LOADING HAS HIS KID HELPING OUT.

THE KID IS LARKING ABOUT AND HAS A BAD ACCIDENT.

WAIT

WA HEY

DANNY!

ALEC · BOOK 4 · Page 19

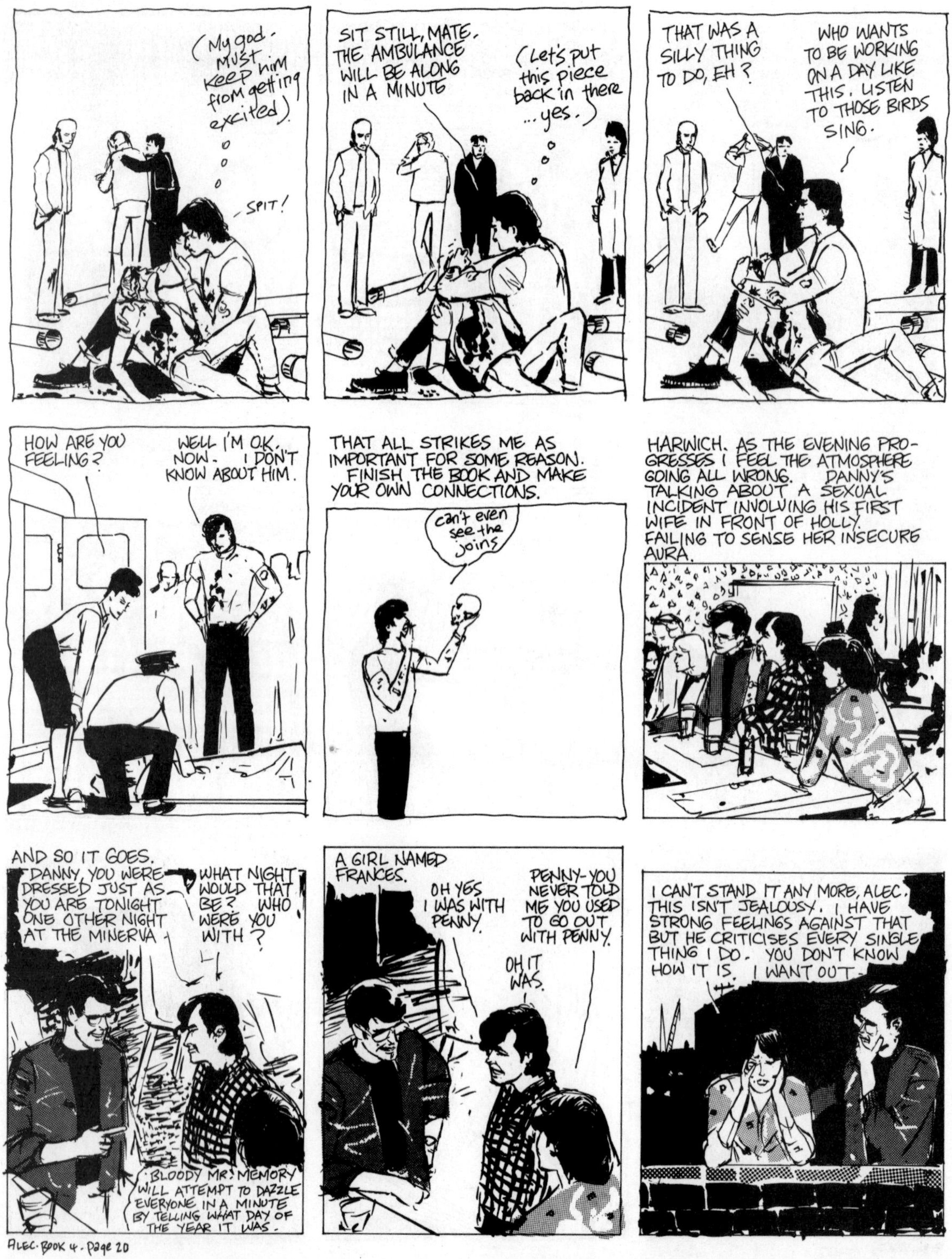
(My god. Must keep him from getting excited)
SPIT!
SIT STILL, MATE. THE AMBULANCE WILL BE ALONG IN A MINUTE
(Let's put this piece back in there ... yes.)
THAT WAS A SILLY THING TO DO, EH?
WHO WANTS TO BE WORKING ON A DAY LIKE THIS. LISTEN TO THOSE BIRDS SING.
HOW ARE YOU FEELING?
WELL I'M O.K. NOW. I DON'T KNOW ABOUT HIM.
THAT ALL STRIKES ME AS IMPORTANT FOR SOME REASON. FINISH THE BOOK AND MAKE YOUR OWN CONNECTIONS.
can't even see the joins
HARWICH. AS THE EVENING PROGRESSES I FEEL THE ATMOSPHERE GOING ALL WRONG. DANNY'S TALKING ABOUT A SEXUAL INCIDENT INVOLVING HIS FIRST WIFE IN FRONT OF HOLLY. FAILING TO SENSE HER INSECURE AURA.
AND SO IT GOES.
DANNY, YOU WERE DRESSED JUST AS YOU ARE TONIGHT ONE OTHER NIGHT AT THE MINERVA
WHAT NIGHT WOULD THAT BE? WHO WERE YOU WITH?
BLOODY MR. MEMORY WILL ATTEMPT TO DAZZLE EVERYONE IN A MINUTE BY TELLING WHAT DAY OF THE YEAR IT WAS.
A GIRL NAMED FRANCES.
OH YES I WAS WITH PENNY.
PENNY-YOU NEVER TOLD ME YOU USED TO GO OUT WITH PENNY.
OH IT WAS.
I CAN'T STAND IT ANY MORE, ALEC. THIS ISN'T JEALOUSY. I HAVE STRONG FEELINGS AGAINST THAT BUT HE CRITICISES EVERY SINGLE THING I DO. YOU DON'T KNOW HOW IT IS. I WANT OUT.

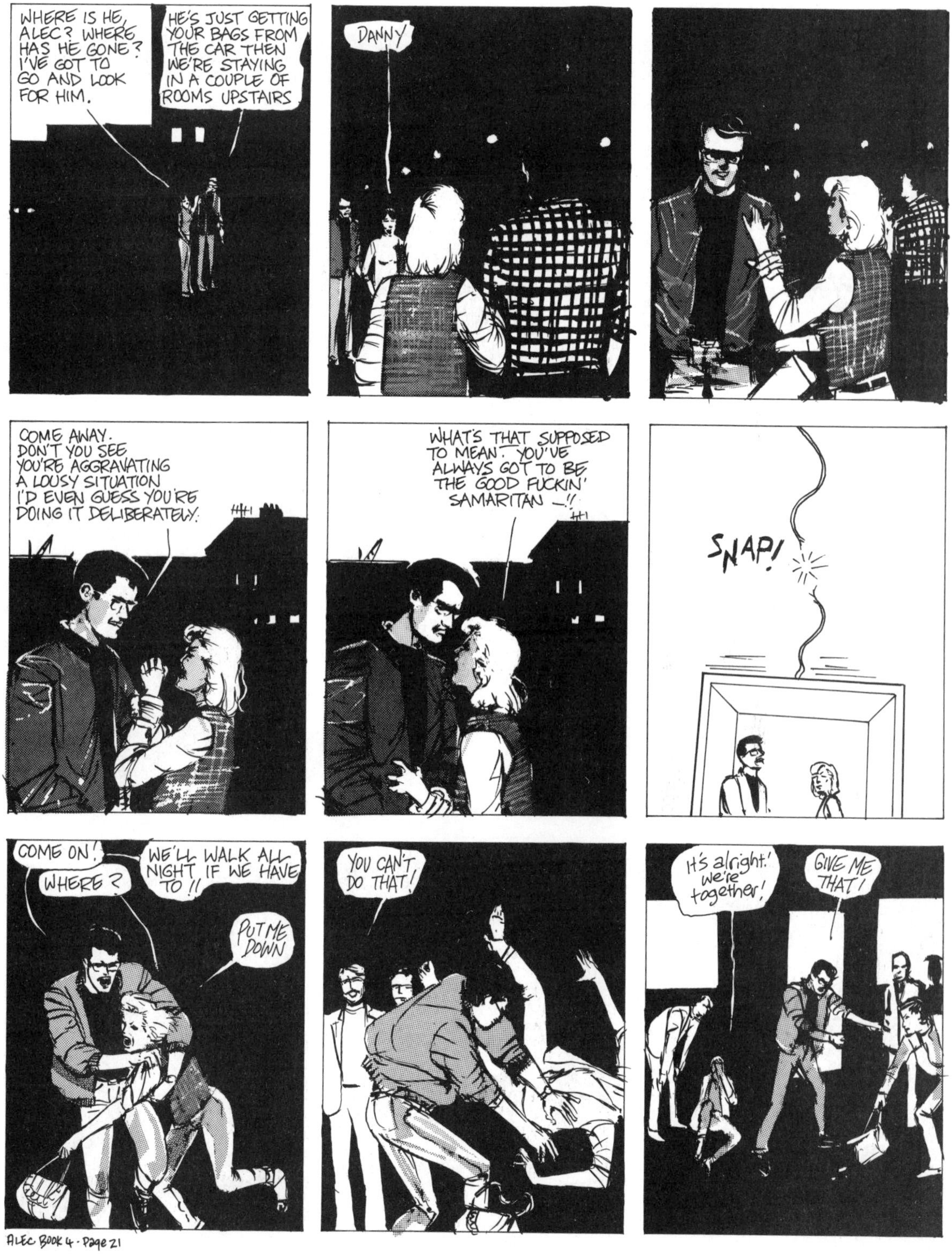
WHERE IS HE, ALEC? WHERE HAS HE GONE? I'VE GOT TO GO AND LOOK FOR HIM.
HE'S JUST GETTING YOUR BAGS FROM THE CAR THEN WE'RE STAYING IN A COUPLE OF ROOMS UPSTAIRS
DANNY
COME AWAY. DON'T YOU SEE YOU'RE AGGRAVATING A LOUSY SITUATION I'D EVEN GUESS YOU'RE DOING IT DELIBERATELY.
WHAT'S THAT SUPPOSED TO MEAN. YOU'VE ALWAYS GOT TO BE THE GOOD FUCKIN' SAMARITAN —!!
SNAP!
COME ON!
WHERE?
WE'LL WALK ALL NIGHT IF WE HAVE TO!!
PUT ME DOWN
YOU CAN'T DO THAT!
It's alright! we're together!
GIVE ME THAT!

I WARNED YOU. I'D DO THIS THE NEXT TIME YOU THREW A JEALOUS FIT!!

YOU FLATTER YOURSELF!! WHAT'S THE POINT IN US? EH? YOU'RE JUST PASSING THE TIME!

IT'S FUNNY HOW IN CRAZY SITUATIONS THE MOST TRIVIAL AND IRRELEVANT DETAIL WILL STICK IN YOUR BRAIN.

AW DAMN

FOR INSTANCE. I USE UP A LOT OF DRAWING PENCILS AND WHEN THEY GET TOO SHORT FOR ME TO HOLD COMFORTABLY I GIVE THEM TO PENNY FOR HER LITTLE GIRL.

There's another pencil

TA

SO HERE I AM AT THE DOCKSIDE IN HARWICH PICKING UP THE SPILLED CONTENTS OF PENNY MOORE'S HANDBAG, ALL THE USUAL STUFF - HAIRSPRAY, COMBS, LIPSTICKS, MINT SWEETS AND ABOUT FIFTEEN 2-INCH PENCILS.

DANNY APPEARS — THE PUB LANDLORD IS EAGER TO CLOSE UP AND GET TO BED.

I AM EAGER MYSELF TO ESCAPE INTO SLEEP FROM THIS POINTLESSNESS.

COME ON, ALEC

THE ADVENTURES ARE OVER. IT IS TIME TO RETURN TO THE HUMDRUM FAMILIAR BEHAVIOUR OF REAL LIFE.

BUT I AWAKE AT HALF PAST MIDNIGHT TO SEE DANNY GREY URINATING INTO PENNY MOORE'S CELEBRATED HANDBAG.

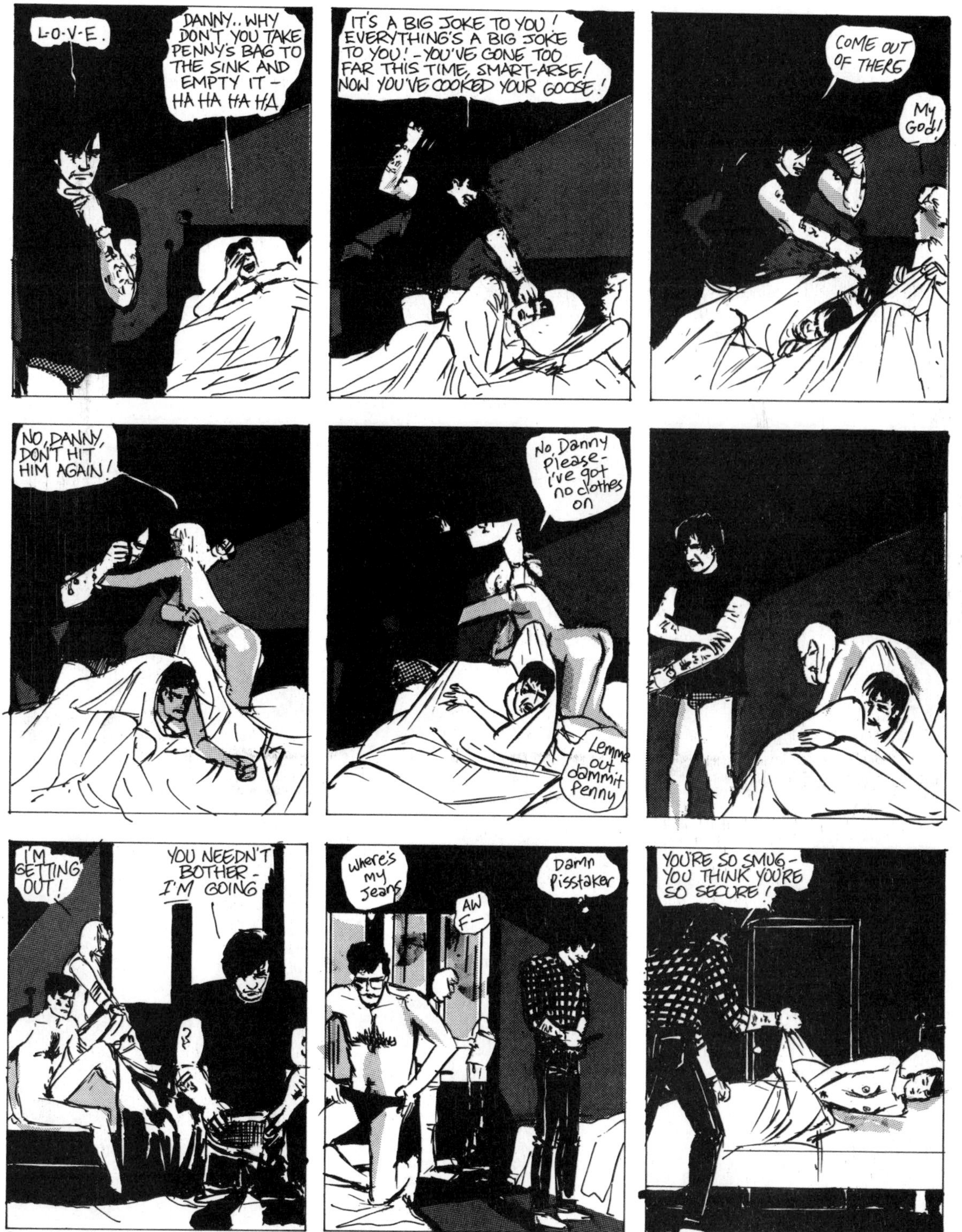
L-O-V-E.
DANNY.. WHY DON'T YOU TAKE PENNY'S BAG TO THE SINK AND EMPTY IT - HA HA HA HA
IT'S A BIG JOKE TO YOU! EVERYTHING'S A BIG JOKE TO YOU! - YOU'VE GONE TOO FAR THIS TIME, SMART-ARSE! NOW YOU'VE COOKED YOUR GOOSE!
COME OUT OF THERE
My God!
NO, DANNY, DON'T HIT HIM AGAIN!
No, Danny Please - I've got no clothes on
Lemme out dammit Penny
I'M GETTING OUT!
YOU NEEDN'T BOTHER - I'M GOING
Where's my Jeans
AW F—
Damn Pisstaker
YOU'RE SO SMUG - YOU THINK YOU'RE SO SECURE!

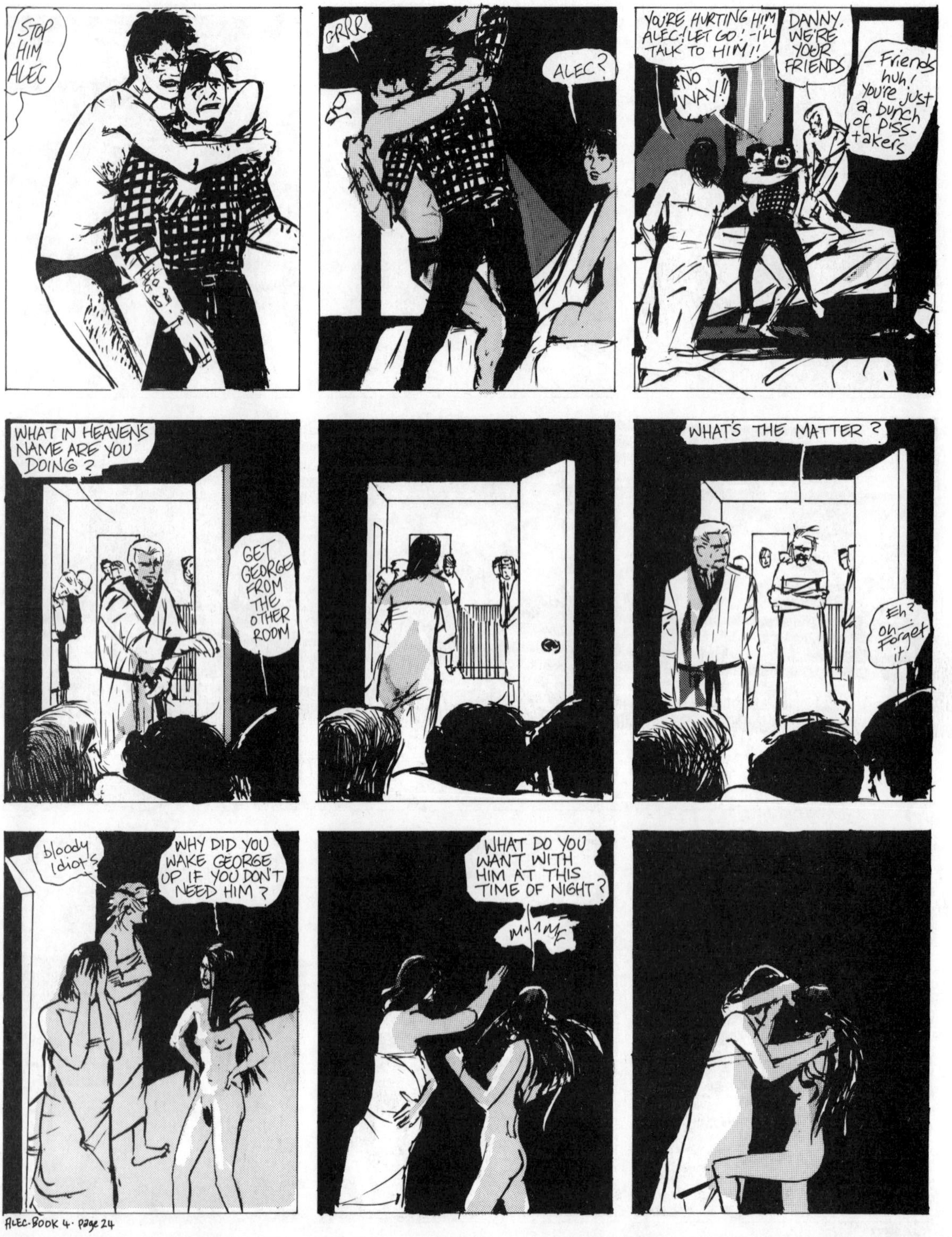
STOP HIM ALEC
GRRR
ALEC?
YOU'RE HURTING HIM ALEC!-LET GO! -I'LL TALK TO HIM!!
NO WAY!!
DANNY, WE'RE YOUR FRIENDS
—Friends huh! You're just a bunch of piss-takers
WHAT IN HEAVEN'S NAME ARE YOU DOING?
GET GEORGE FROM THE OTHER ROOM
WHAT'S THE MATTER?
Eh? Oh— Forget it.
bloody idiots
WHY DID YOU WAKE GEORGE UP IF YOU DON'T NEED HIM?
WHAT DO YOU WANT WITH HIM AT THIS TIME OF NIGHT?

SKREEE

Tom hasn't noticed the piss on the floor

Bloody Roman orgy

Poor Danny

I HOPE HE PAID YOU IN ADVANCE

IN THE MORNING IT'S A BIG SHARED HANGOVER. GEORGE REGRETS BEING RATTY.

ALEC- CAN YOU GO BACK FOR MY WATCH

I'LL GET IT

DANNY AND ALEC DON'T SPEAK TO EACH OTHER FOR A WHOLE YEAR, MAINLY DUE TO EMBARRASSMENT.

AH, IF WE COULD SEE THE FUTURE, FIVE YEARS AFTER THIS, GEORGE WAITE AND PENNY MOORE GET MARRIED FOR A WHILE.

ME, TODAY.. I'M ON THE OTHER SIDE OF THE WORLD RIDING A GREYHOUND DOWN TO BRISBANE TO TRY TO FIND WORK, A FORD FAIRLANE PASSES WITH A DOGGIE IN THE BACK SEAT-- WATCHING ME THROUGH THE WINDOW -

SHOULD I LAY ME DOWN FOR KEEPS, BEFORE WHAT'S GRIM MY SPIRIT REAPS,

HOLD FOR ME A LITTLE WAKE AND DROWN IN WHAT THE BREWERS MAKE.

WHEN MY TIME COMES, WHEN I RATTLE MY CLACK,

WHEN I KICK THE BUCKET,

FALL INTO THE CRACK,

SAY SOME WORDS BUT KEEP IT BRIEF.

THEN ALL SING ALONG TO MY FAVOURITE TRACK ("I CAN'T GET STARTED" by BUNNY BERIGAN and his orchestra, 1938.)

Life goes on ... the book stops here ———— *Eddie Campbell* NTH, Queensland '87